2nd EDITION

INCREDIBLE ENGLISH

Class Book

4

Peter Redpath

Kirstie Grainger   Michaela Morgan   Sarah Phillips

OXFORD
UNIVERSITY PRESS

THE INCREDIBLE CLUB

1 **Listen and find.** 🔊 1.1

Name: Archie Taylor
Age: 8
Birthday: 29th October
Phone number: 783066

Name: Finn Cooper
Age: 9
Birthday: 3rd February
Phone number: 814452

Name: Jazmin Patel
Age: 9
Birthday: 13th June
Phone number: 759163

Name: Molly Finch
Age: 8
Birthday: 31st July
Phone number: 820781

Name: Luke Finch
Age: 10
Birthday: 22nd April
Phone number: 820781

Name: Eve Wilkins
Age: 18
Birthday: 8th January
Phone number: 704956

2 **Ask and answer.**

What's her name?

It's Eve Wilkins.

How old is she?

She's eighteen.

When's her birthday?

It's on the eighth of January.

What's her phone number?

It's 704956.

1 At the adventure camp

1 Look, listen and repeat. 1.2

2 Listen and find. 1.3

1 play tennis   **2** fish   **3** waterski   **4** sail   **5** row   **6** swim   **7** climb

8 play hide and seek   **9** rollerblade   **10** play football   **11** play basketball   **12** skateboard

3 Ask and answer.

Can you waterski?

Yes, I can.

Can you play tennis?

No, I can't.

1 Listen and read. 🎧 1.5

A busy week

2 Read and write the number.

a   Jazmin wants to play tennis.

b   Luke and Finn want to
    go climbing.

c   Eve wants to go rollerblading.

d   The children want to go sailing.

e   Luke and Finn want to go
    swimming.

f   Molly wants to go climbing.

g   The children want to have
    a rest!

h   Archie wants to go fishing.

3 Complete with one word.

1   Finn wants to go swimming. He's ___hot___ .

2   The girls don't want to go fishing.
    It's too _____ .

3   Eve doesn't want to go sailing. She's _____ .

4   The children don't want to go rollerblading.
    They're _____ .

4 Listen again and act. 1.5

1 Which sentence is in the story? Make more sentences.

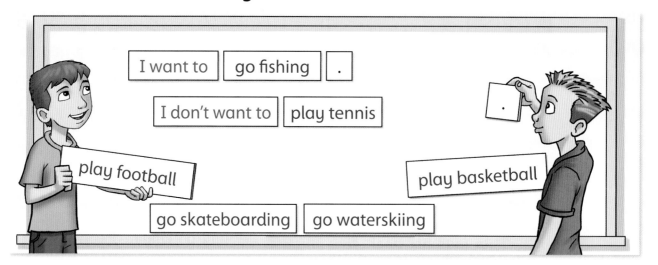

I want to | go fishing | .

I don't want to | play tennis

play football

play basketball

go skateboarding | go waterskiing

2 Listen and say which day is best. 1.6

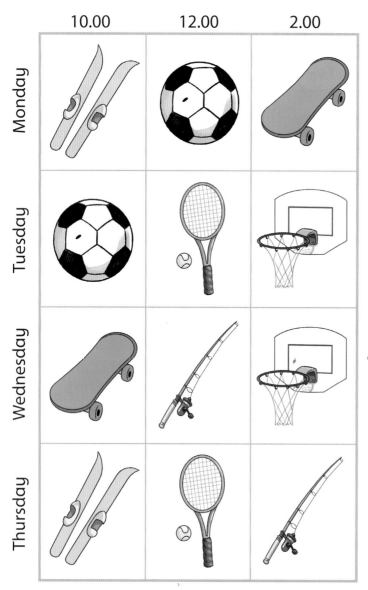

	10.00	12.00	2.00
Monday			
Tuesday			
Wednesday			
Thursday			

3 Play the game.

I want to play tennis.

OK.

I don't want to go fishing.

Right!

Which day is best for me?

Tuesday.

Thank you!

4 Complete. Then choose a day and write two paragraphs for your partner to complete.

1 I want to play basketball, but I don't want to play tennis. The best day for me is _____ .

2 I want to go waterskiing, but I don't want to go fishing. The best day for me is _____ .

1 Look and read quickly. Who writes about these activities: *Luke* or *Eve*?

 a

 b

 c

To: finchfamily@mymail.co.uk

Subject: **Hello!**

Dear Mum and Dad,

I'm having a fantastic time at the adventure camp. There are lots of things to do. I go fishing with Archie, and I sometimes play tennis with Eve. There's a big swimming pool, and a **lake** where you can go rowing and sailing. I like sailing, but my favourite activity is climbing. There's a big climbing **wall**. It's scary but it's brilliant!

I'm sleeping in a tent with Archie and Finn. It's very comfortable!

Love from Luke

To: jimandbetty@onemail.co.uk

Subject: **Having fun!**

Dear Mum and Dad,

I love the adventure camp. The countryside is beautiful, and you can do so many sports and activities! There's a tennis **court** and a basketball **court**, and a  big football **pitch**. There's a volleyball **court** too. I'm learning to play volleyball. I like it but I'm not very good at it!

The activities are great fun, but I'm very tired. The children always want to get up so early!

See you soon.

Love from Eve

2 Read the emails again and answer *Yes* or *No*.

1 Is there a swimming pool at the camp? _____

2 Does Luke go fishing at the camp? _____

3 Is he sleeping in a hotel? _____

4 Does Eve like the adventure camp? _____

5 Is she learning to play football? _____

6 Do the children want to get up early? _____

3 Complete with the underlined words from the text.

1 Where can you play basketball? On a basketball *court* .

2 Where can you climb? On a climbing *wall* .

3 Where can you play football? On a football *pitch* .

4 Where can you go sailing? On a *lake* .

The water cycle and the weather

1 Look and read.

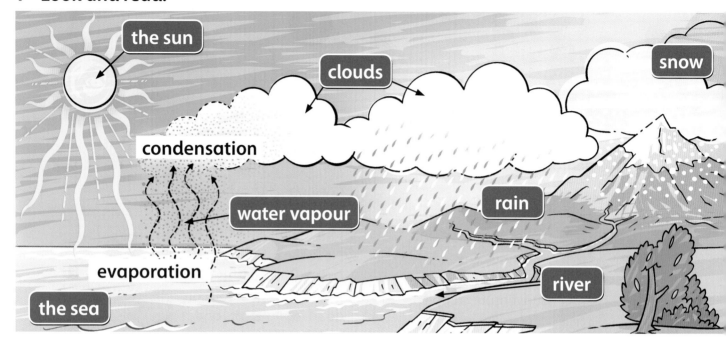

2 Listen, read and find. 1.10

Rain comes from the water in the sea. First, the sun shines on the sea. It warms the water. Can you find this?

The water becomes water vapour. This process is called evaporation. The wind carries the water vapour up into the sky. Can you find this?

High in the sky the air is cooler. When the water vapour meets the cooler air, it becomes very small drops of water that form clouds. This process is called condensation. Can you find this?

The small drops of water join together and become rain drops. The raindrops are bigger and heavier than the clouds and fall to the ground. It's raining! Can you find this?

If it's very cold or high in the mountains, it snows. Can you find this?
The rain and snow falls into the rivers and the rivers carry the water back to the sea. And it starts all over again! This is the water cycle.

3 Read and choose.

1 It shines on the sea.   water vapour / the sun
2 It becomes clouds.   the sun / water vapour
3 It becomes rain.   small water drops / cool air
4 The air is cooler here.   high in the sky / near the sun
5 It carries the water to the sea.   a cloud / a river

1 Look, listen and repeat. 🔊 1.11   2 Listen and find. 🔊 1.12

a It's sunny.

b It's cloudy.

c It's windy.

d It's raining.

e It's snowing.

f FOG It's foggy.

g It's stormy.

h +10°C It's 10 degrees.

i −5°C It's minus 5.

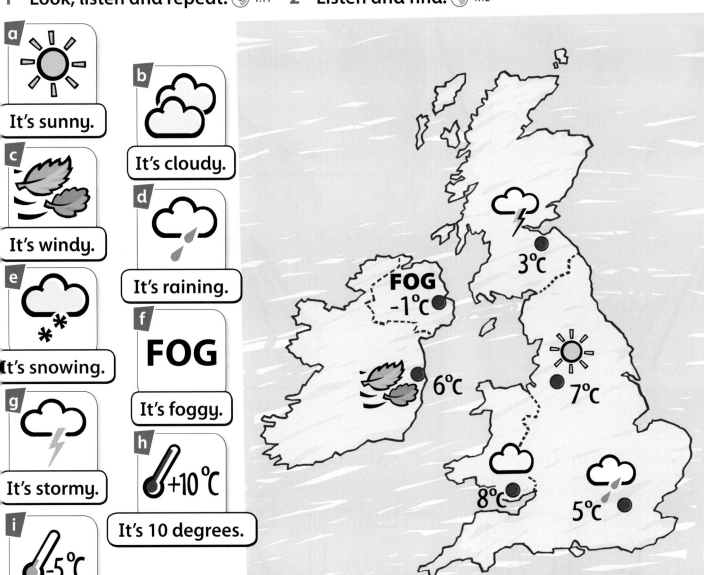

FOG −1°C

3°C

6°C

7°C

8°C

5°C

3 Ask and answer.

What's the weather like in Cardiff?

It's cloudy.

What's the temperature?

It's eight degrees.

Talk about it!

What's the weather like in Cardiff?	Manchester Dublin Edinburgh Belfast London
It's cloudy.	windy snowing raining sunny stormy foggy
What's the temperature?	
It's eight degrees.	minus five

1 Make a weather map.

2 Colour.

1 Draw and write.

3 Write.

1 Listen, find and repeat.  1.13　2 Listen and say the chant. 1.14

Chant

sk	sw	sn	sl	st
			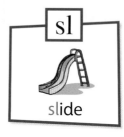	
scooter	swing	snow	slide	standing

Playing on a red swing,
Sliding down a slide,
Standing on a climbing frame
Up so high!

Playing on a scooter,
Skiing in the snow,
Swimming in the water,
Here we go!

2 Art

1 Look, listen and repeat. 1.15

2 Listen and find. 1.16

1 teacher   2 dancer   3 astronaut   4 artist   5 scientist   6 policeman
7 pilot   8 doctor   9 actor   10 pirate   11 footballer   12 firefighter

3 Ask and answer.

behind   next to
in front of   under   on

Where's Luke?

He's next to the footballer.

1 Listen and read. 🎧 1.18

Art Day

1 It's Art Day at the club!

I need some paint.

Can I have a brush, please?

I want to draw, but I haven't got any ideas!

2 Don't worry. Anna is coming. She's an artist and a teacher. She can help!

3 Anna's late. She's never late! She always gets up at six o'clock.

That's very early! I get up at seven o'clock.

4 Meanwhile, on the road ...

I need to get to the club for Art Day, and I'm late. Oh!

Oh no! What a mess!

2 Complete the summary.

The children are at the ¹ __.
It's Art Day, but they haven't got
any ² __. Anna is a teacher and an
³ __. She can help but she is ⁴ __.
She falls off her bike. Eve and the
children go for a ⁵ __ and they
see Anna. Molly has an ⁶ __. The
children paint the bike!

3 Answer. Write one word.

1 Who wants a brush? _____
2 Who always gets up at six o'clock? _____
3 What time does Molly get up?
   At _____ o'clock.
4 Who wants to go for a walk? _____
5 Who do they see? _____
6 What do the children paint? The _____.

4 Listen again and act. 1.18

1 Which sentence is in the story? Make more sentences.

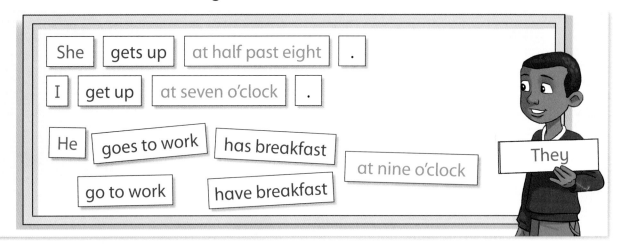

| She | gets up | at half past eight | . |

| I | get up | at seven o'clock | . |

He | goes to work | has breakfast | at nine o'clock | They
go to work | have breakfast

2 Listen and say which pair of people. 1.19

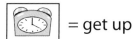 = get up

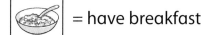 = have breakfast

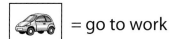 = go to work

3 Play the game.

She gets up at half past seven.

OK.

They go to work at half past eight.

I know Mr and Mrs Smith.

That's right!

4 Complete. Then write four sentences for your partner to complete.

1 Mr and Mrs _____ have breakfast at eight o'clock.

2 Mr _____ goes to work at half past eight.

1 **Look. Guess which words are in the interview? Read and check.**

| **1** comics | **2** computer | **3** cake | **4** bicycles | **5** art gallery |

An interview with

Jed Smith

Jed Smith is an artist. Here we ask him some questions about his life.

Where do you live?
I live in London, with my <u>wife</u>, Sally.

What kind of art do you do?
I'm a cartoonist – I draw cartoons for comics. I love drawing <u>funny</u> pictures.

Do you write the cartoon stories as well?
No, my friend is a writer and she writes the stories. I read her stories and then draw

the people in the story. I like reading cartoon stories, even though I'm 32 years old!

Is it difficult to draw cartoons?
Sometimes – I think drawing animals is quite difficult. I like drawing people best. I don't draw on paper, I draw on a computer and I have lots of computer programmes to help me.

When do you work?
I like working in the mornings, before breakfast. I get up very early. I don't like

working in the evenings. I like cooking and <u>relaxing</u> in the evenings.

What do you do at the weekend?
Sally and I have got bicycles and we often go <u>cycling</u> on Saturdays. And we love going to the cinema.

2 **Read the interview again and answer** *Yes* **or** *No*.

1 Is Jed a teacher?
2 Does he write cartoon stories?
3 Does he draw on a computer?

4 Does he work in the evenings?
5 Does he like cooking?
6 Has he got a bicycle?

3 **Find these words in the text.**

Draw with a grid

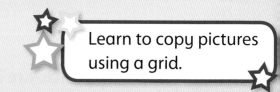
Learn to copy pictures using a grid.

1 **Look, listen and repeat.** 1.23

2 **Listen and find.** 1.24

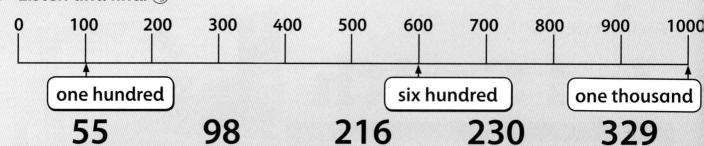

| 0 | 100 | 200 | 300 | 400 | 500 | 600 | 700 | 800 | 900 | 1000 |

one hundred **six hundred** **one thousand**

55 **98** **216** **230** **329**

The Sapphire Building, Istanbul, Turkey. Built in **2010. 216** m high.

Leaning tower of Pisa, Italy. Built **1173-1350**. It is **55** m high.

Big Ben, London, England. Built in **1858**. It is **98** m high.

Be careful! We say dates and numbers differently:

1,975 = one thousand, nine hundred and seventy-five

1975 = nineteen seventy-five

Here are some more dates:

1173 = eleven seventy-three

2019 = twenty nineteen

The Palace of Science and Culture, Warsaw, Poland. Built **1953-1955**. It is **230** m high.

The Eiffel Tower, Paris, France. Built in **1889**. It is **329** m high.

Buildings

1 Ask and answer

Talk about it!

Tell me about this tower.

It's **216** metres high. 230 329 55 98

It's 216 metres high. It was built in 2010. It's in Turkey. It's the Sapphire Building.

It was **built** in **2010**. between **1173** and **1350**
between **1953** and **1955**
in **1858**, in **1889**

It's in Turkey. Poland England France Italy

2 Look at the pictures. Read and order the texts to match the pictures.

3 Listen and check. 🔊 1.26

Finish your drawing and colour it. Now you have a picture of the Eiffel Tower. ☐

Now copy the lines of the tower in each small square. ☐

First find a photo. This is a photo of the Eiffel Tower. Draw a grid on the photo. This grid has got 20 squares. ☐

Now draw the same grid on a big piece of paper. If you want to make your picture bigger than your photo, draw a bigger grid. ☐

1

2

3

4

1 Copy a drawing with a grid.

1 **Draw a grid on the picture.**

2 **Copy the grid.**

3 **Copy the picture.**

4 **Colour and write.**

1 Listen, find and repeat. 🎧 1.27   **2 Listen and say the chant.** 🎧 1.28

Chant

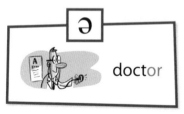

ə

doctor

Soldier, sailor,
Singer, dancer,
Policeman,
Postman,
Fireman,
Chief!

Doctor, actor,
Pilot, pirate,
Policeman,
Postman,
Fireman,
Chief!

3 Feeling great

1 **Look, listen and repeat.** 🔊 1.29

2 **Listen and find.** 🔊 1.30

I've got ...   **1** an earache.   **2** a stomach ache.   **3** a cough.

4 a cold.   **6** a toothache.   **8** a sore throat.   **9** a headache.

I feel ...

5 sick.   **7** dizzy.

3 **Ask and answer.**

> What's the matter?

> I've got a cold.

> What's the matter?

> I feel dizzy.

1 Listen and read. 🔊 1.32

The concert

2 Complete the summary.

Eve and the children are going to a ¹_____ . They are ²_____ because there is a traffic jam. They stop so Molly can drink some ³_____ . Then they see Suzy Silver. There is a problem with her ⁴_____ so they give her a lift. The children are very excited. ⁵_____ gets them seats at the front. The concert is ⁶_____ !

3 Look at the story and correct one word.

3 Archie has got a ~~toothache~~. *headache*

4 Jazmin gives Finn some water.

6 Molly can do all of Suzy's songs.

8 Eve says the concert is boring.

9 Eve feels tired.

10 Luke says Coco should sit still.

4 Listen again and act. 1.32

1 **Which sentence is in the story? Make more sentences.**

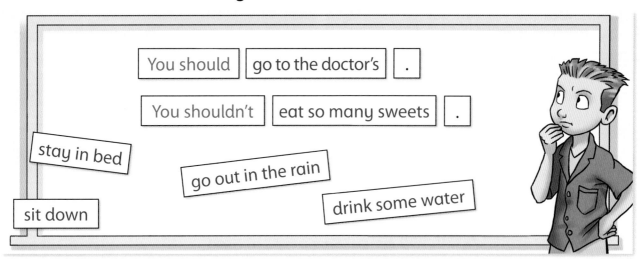

You should | go to the doctor's | .

You shouldn't | eat so many sweets | .

stay in bed

go out in the rain

sit down

drink some water

2 **Listen and say which picture.** 1.33

3 **Look and say.**

I've got a cold.

You should stay in bed.

I feel sick.

You shouldn't eat so many sweets.

4 **Complete. Then write two sentences for your partner to complete.**

1 If you feel dizzy, you should _____ .

2 If you've got a cold, you shouldn't _____ .

3 If you've got an earache, you should _____ .

1 Look and read quickly. Match the rules to the pictures.

Four rules for healthy living

Your health is very important! Here are four rules to keep you healthy:

1 **Eat healthy food.** It's a good idea to eat five portions of fruit and vegetables every day. Don't eat lots of <u>junk food</u>. If you feel hungry between meals, eat an an apple or a banana.

2 **Drink lots of water.** Your body is 70% water, so it needs lots of water to keep it healthy. You should drink six to eight glasses of water every day. Don't drink lots of <u>sweet</u> drinks because the sugar is bad for your teeth.

3 **Get enough sleep.** Your body needs to <u>rest</u> every day. Most adults need seven or eight hours of sleep every night, and children need more. Don't be tired!

4 **Do some <u>exercise</u> every day.** You can go for a walk, go swimming or play football. You need exercise because it makes you strong and it's good for your heart. And it makes you feel good too!

a
b
c
d

2 Read the poster again and answer.

1 How many portions of fruit and vegetables should we eat every day?

2 How much of your body is water?

3 Why shouldn't you drink lots of sweet drinks?

4 How much sleep do adults need?

5 How often should we do exercise?

3 Complete with the underlined words from the text.

1 When we sleep or _____ , our body stops moving.

2 A _____ drink has got lots of sugar in it.

3 Hamburgers, chips and sweets are not healthy food. They are _____ .

4 Dancing, tennis and running are different kinds of _____ .

Pulse rates

  Learn about pulse rates and how to take your pulse.

1 Look, listen and repeat. 🔊 1.37   **2 Listen, read and answer.** 🔊 1.38

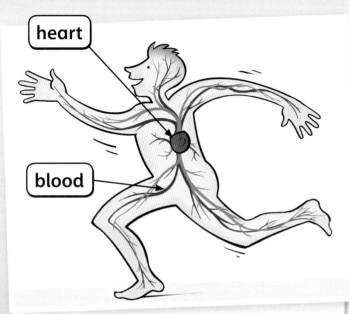

heart

blood

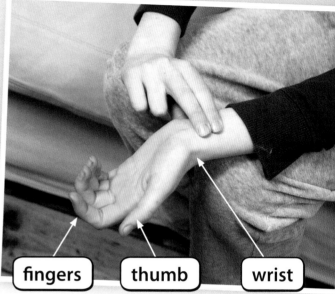

fingers   thumb   wrist

Your heart pumps blood around your body. Your heart usually beats about 70 times per minute. When you do a lot of exercise, your heart works more and so it beats more.

You can feel these heartbeats. Put two fingers under the thumb on your left wrist. Press your wrist gently with your fingers. This is your pulse. You measure your pulse in beats per minute (BPM). Take your pulse for 10 seconds. How many beats? Now multiply this number by 6. How many beats per minute is your pulse?

3 Read and match.

Time	7.00	7.30	8.00
A	150 BPM	70 BPM	100 BPM
B	70 BPM	75 BPM	80 BPM
C	65 BPM	70 BPM	150 BPM

2 Milly reads in bed at seven o'clock. She gets up and has breakfast at 7.30. At eight o'clock she runs to school. She's always late!

1 Olga gets up early and goes running at seven o'clock. Then at 7.30 she has breakfast and watches TV. At eight o'clock she goes to school. She walks to school.

3 Josh has breakfast at seven o'clock. At 7.30 he gets dressed. At eight o'clock he takes the bus to school.

Hand and heart

1 Listen and find. 🎵 1.39

1 MWW 68 BPM MWW

2 MWW 97 BPM MWW

3 MWW 140 BPM MWW

4 MWW 120 BPM MWW

5 MWW 89 BPM MWW

6 MWW 78 BPM MWW

2 Ask and answer.

What's her pulse after playing football?

It's 120.

Talk about it!

What's her pulse after
sleeping?

playing football?
walking to school?
skipping?
playing computer games?
reading?

It's 68.   97 140 120 89 78

1 Make a BPM chart.

1 Take your pulse.

2 Do the activity for one minute.

3 Write.

1 Listen, find and repeat. 🔊 1.40   2 Listen and say the chant. 🔊 1.41   Chant

tʃ

chicken

It's party time, so wash your hands.
We're eating in the kitchen.
Come on, children,
Hurry up!
There's fish and chips and chicken!

Take off your shoes and find a chair,
And choose the dish for you.
There's fish and chips
And chicken and chips,
And chocolate cheesecake too!

ʃ

shoes

Me and my world

1 **Look. Guess which words are in the text.** ✏️ **Read and check.**

1 / island **2** / ocean **3** / foggy **4** / desert **5** / funny **6** / seeds **7** / skiing

Hi, my name's Lilja. I live in Iceland. Iceland is a big island in the North Atlantic Ocean. It is very cold here in winter and it is never very hot in summer. But in one day you can see many different types of weather.

Last year I was climbing a volcano, Hekla. It was sunny when we started. It was foggy at the top and there was some snow. It was raining and windy when we climbed down. People in Iceland say "You shouldn't worry about the weather. It changes every five minutes!" I think this is true!

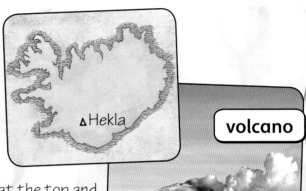

▲Hekla

volcano

My name's Paul. I'm from South Africa. Last year I visited the Kalahari Desert. It is usually dry and hot there. The sand is red and the wind forms it into fantastic shapes.

A lot of plants and animals live in the Kalahari. My favourite animals were the meerkats. They live in big family groups. We watched them play together. They were very funny!

One day it rained and the next day was amazing. Everything was green! Our guide explained that the seeds wait in the sand, and when there is water they grow as quickly as they can.

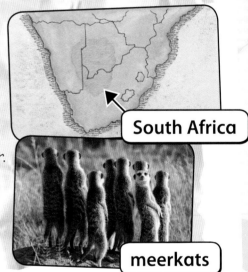

South Africa

meerkats

2 **Read again and answer the questions.** ✏️

1 Where is Iceland?

2 What's the weather like in summer?

3 What's the weather like in winter?

4 What was the weather like at the top of Hekla?

5 Where is the Kalahari Desert?

6 What colour is the sand?

7 Do any animals live in the Kalahari?

8 What happens when it rains?

 **Revision**  Play the game!

 Say
 Ask and answer
 Sing a song
 W Say a word beginning with these letters
Talk about it

1 Play in pairs. You need 3 counters each.

2 Put your counter on a square and follow the instructions.

3 Take turns.

4 Make a line of 3 to win!

Learning to learn – Finding words

 cloud

1 Look at the first letter. Find the right page in your dictionary.

2 Look at the second and third letters to help you find the word.

3 Can you put these words in dictionary order?

scientist   stomach ache   sick   stormy   stairs   sail

4 At school

1 Look, listen and repeat. 2.1

2 Listen and find. 2.2

1 poster **2** P.E. **3** Science **4** Spanish **5** History **6** English
7 classroom **8** Music **9** Maths **10** Geography **11** Art

3 Ask and answer.

Which do you prefer, Maths or Music?

Music.

1 Listen and read. 2.4

The good old days

1 It's Sports Day at school.

Come on, Dad. I don't want to be late.

OK, I'm coming ... oh look, there's my old teacher, Mr Simpson!

2 Were you good at school?

I was good at History. My favourite topic was Ancient Egypt.

3 I wasn't very good at Maths.

Oh! Maths is my favourite subject.

4 What about school lunches, Dad?

Oh, they were terrible.

5 The teachers were very strict when I was a boy.

6 Was there a Sports Day, Dad? Were you good at P.E.?

Yes, there was. I was very good at P.E.!

2 Read and write *True* or *False*.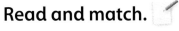

1 It's Art Day at school.
2 Mr Simpson was Finn's dad's teacher.
3 Finn's dad was good at Maths.

4 School lunches were great.
5 The teachers were very strict.
6 Finn's dad won a medal at Sports Day.

3 Read and match.

1 Finn's dad sees his old teacher
2 He was good at History,
3 He tells Finn and Jazmin
4 He was the only runner

a but he wasn't good at Maths.
b because everybody was sick.
c when they arrive at school.
d about his medal at Sports Day.

4 Listen again and act. 2.4

1   Which sentence is in the story? Make more sentences.

2   Listen and say who. 2.5

	Maths	Science	Art	History
Jazmin's dad	✔	✘	✔	✘
Finn's dad	✘	✘	✔	✔
Mr Simpson	✘	✔	✘	✔
Archie's dad	✔	✔	✘	✘

3   Play the game.

4   Write *True* or *False*. Then write four true or false sentences for your partner.

1   Archie's dad was good at Science.

2   Jazmin's dad wasn't good at Art.

3   Mr Simpson was good at Maths.

4   Finn's dad wasn't good at Science.

1 Look and read quickly. Match the photos to the descriptions.

1

In this photo, I can see about 13 children. They aren't wearing school uniform. Most of them are writing.

The teacher is sitting at the front of the classroom. She is writing on the <u>projector</u>. There is a <u>blackboard</u> on the wall and a map of the world.

I think this is a photo of a classroom in the 1960s.

by Mark

2

In this photo, there are about 6 children. Some of them are sitting down and some of them are standing up. Two of the children are playing the <u>keyboard</u>. I think this is a music lesson.

The children are wearing school uniform. The teacher is at the back of the classroom.

I think this is a photo of a modern classroom.

By Amy

3

In this photo, there are about 18 children. The children are wearing <u>school uniform</u>. They are sitting in rows. There is one desk for each child. All of the children have a notebook on their desk.

The teacher is at the back of the classroom. She is standing up. There are photographs on the wall.

by Tanya, class 5B

2 Look and read again and write *True* or *False*.

1 Tanya's photo shows about 18 children.

2 Mark's photo shows a small classroom.

3 The teacher is at the back of the classroom in Amy's photo.

4 The children in Mark's photo are sitting in rows.

5 All of the children in Amy's photo are standing up.

6 Mark can't see a teacher in his photo.

7 There are photographs on the wall in Tanya's photo.

3 Find these words in the text.

1

2

3

4

Ancient Egypt

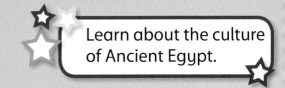
Learn about the culture of Ancient Egypt.

1 Look, listen and repeat. 2.9

mummy

pyramid

god

pharaoh

headdress
goddess

2 Listen, read and answer. 2.10

The River Nile was very important in Ancient Egypt. The Nile is the longest river in the world: it is 6,695 kilometres long. The Ancient Egyptians lived next to the River Nile because the land was good for farming. Can you find the river?

Pharaohs were kings in Ancient Egypt. When they died, the people buried them in tombs. The Ancient Egyptians built pyramids as tombs for the pharaohs and their queens. The three biggest pyramids are at Giza. Can you find Giza on the map?

When pharaohs or other important people died, their bodies were wrapped in special bandages. A body wrapped and buried like this is called a mummy. They last for thousands of years.

The Ancient Egyptians believed in many different gods and goddesses. Each god or goddess was very important in Ancient Egypt. Sometimes the god or goddess had the head of an animal. Can you see a god or goddess with the head of an animal on this page?

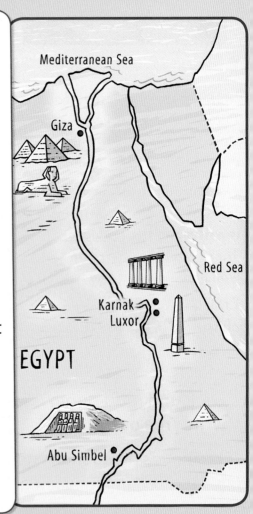
Mediterranean Sea
Giza
Red Sea
Karnak
Luxor
EGYPT
Abu Simbel

3 Read and write *True* or *False*.

1 The River Nile is 6,695 km long.

2 The Nile was important because the land was good for farming.

3 The Pharaoh was the queen of Ancient Egypt.

4 The biggest pyramids are at Giza.

5 The mummies weren't important people.

1 Read. Then listen and find. 🔊 2.11

Osiris was the god of the dead. He was the father of Horus. He had a white headdress with feathers.

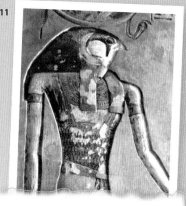

Horus was a god of the sky. He was the son of Isis and Osiris. He had the head of a bird.

Isis was the mother goddess. She was the wife of Osiris and the mother of Horus. She had a headdress of cow horns.

Sobek was a god of the Nile. He had the head of a crocodile and a headdress of feathers.

Bastet was a goddess with the head of a cat. She was a kind goddess. Cats were very important in Ancient Egypt.

Tefnut was the goddess of water. She had the head of a lioness.

2 Ask and answer.

Is it a god? — Yes.

Did he have the head of a bird? — No.

Did he have a headdress of white feathers? — Yes.

Osiris! — Yes!

Talk about it!

Is it a god?   goddess?

Did he/she have   the head of a lioness?
the head of a crocodile?
the head of a cat?
the head of a bird?
a headdress with feathers?
a headdress with cow horns?

1 Make Egyptian pictures.

1 Draw and colour.

2 Write.

1 Listen, find and repeat. 2.12   **2 Listen and say the chant.** 2.13    Chant

θ thumb

f fin

I've got eight fingers,
I've got two thumbs,
I can throw frisbees,
I think it's fun.

Fish don't have fingers,
They've got fins,
Fish can't throw frisbees,
But wow! They can swim!

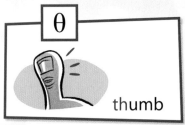

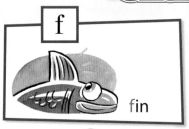

5 At the aquarium

1 Look, listen and repeat. 🔊 2.14
2 Listen and find. 🔊 2.15

1 water	2 shark	3 dolphin	4 boat	5 octopus	6 jellyfish
12 sand	7 fish	8 crab	9 starfish	10 shell	11 seahorse

3 Ask and answer.

How many sharks can you see?

Two.

1 Listen and read. 2.18

Coco was a star!
She played with the dolphin.

But it wasn't a shark.
It was a dolphin!

Hurray! Well
done, Coco!

And at the end of the show she
had fish for lunch. She liked the
fish! We had a great day!

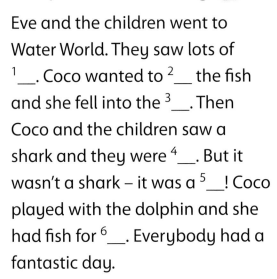

2 Complete the summary.

Eve and the children went to
Water World. They saw lots of
¹__. Coco wanted to ²__ the fish
and she fell into the ³__. Then
Coco and the children saw a
shark and they were ⁴__. But it
wasn't a shark – it was a ⁵__! Coco
played with the dolphin and she
had fish for ⁶__. Everybody had a
fantastic day.

3 Read and write *True* or *False*.

1 Archie had a great time at the aquarium.
2 He saw a seahorse.
3 The children had strawberry ice creams
for lunch.
4 Coco wanted to eat egg and chips.
5 Coco fell into the water.
6 She wasn't scared.
7 She played with a shark.
8 She liked her lunch.

4 Listen again and act. 2.18

1 Which sentence is in the story? Make more sentences.

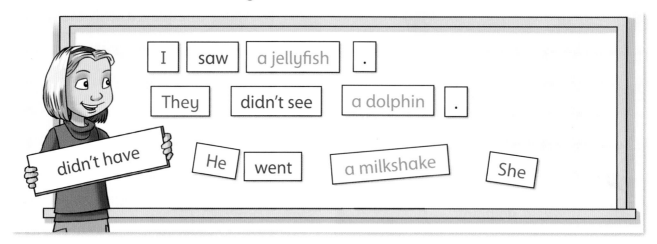

I | saw | a jellyfish | .

They | didn't see | a dolphin | .

didn't have

He | went | a milkshake | She

2 Listen and say which girl. 2.19

3 Play the game.

She didn't go to the beach.
She went to Water World.

OK.

She didn't see a jellyfish.
She saw a dolphin.

Go on.

She didn't have an ice cream.
She had a milkshake

Yes!

Number 5?

4 Read and say which girl. Then write six sentences about a different girl.

She didn't go to Water World. She went to the beach.

She didn't see a dolphin. She saw a jellyfish.

She didn't have an ice cream. She had a milkshake.

1 Look. Guess which words are in the leaflet? Read and check.

| 1 starfish | 2 dolphins | 3 children | 4 fish and chips | 5 books |

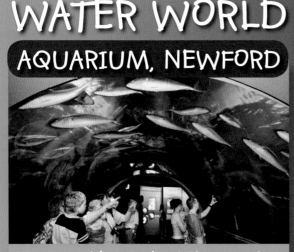

WATER WORLD
AQUARIUM, NEWFORD

Come and learn about the amazing world under the sea!

Did you know that there are more than 29,000 <u>species</u> of fish in the world? At Water World you can walk in our underwater tunnels and see fish swim past your nose! You can see sharks, crabs, jellyfish and lots more.

1

In the three outdoor pools, you can watch dolphins and <u>seals</u> jumping and playing. Visit the big pool at 11am and 2pm and you can help feed the animals.

NEW! There is a Water World beach with real sand, where children can <u>splash</u> in the water and make <u>sandcastles</u>. Don't forget your towel and your swimming costume!

There are lots of souvenirs in the Water World shop. You can buy our DVD, 'Water World magic', posters of your favourite fish, and lots more.

At the Water World Café there is a variety of delicious hot and cold food. Try our special meal: fish and chips and chocolate ice cream!

Water World – A great day out for all the family!

2

2 Read the leaflet again and answer.

1 What town is Water World in?
2 How many species of fish are there in the world?
3 How many outdoor pools are there at Water World?
4 What animals can you see in the outdoor pools?
5 Where can you feed the animals?
6 What can children do at the beach?
7 What is the name of the DVD?
8 What special meal can you buy at the café?

3 Complete with the underlined words from the text.

1 _____ are animals that swim and eat fish.
2 I jumped into the swimming pool and made a big _____ .
3 There are many_____ of fish.
4 We make _____ at the beach.

Fish

1 Look, listen and repeat. 2.23

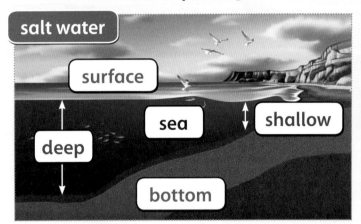

salt water

surface

sea

shallow

deep

bottom

fresh water

lake

river

2 Do the quiz. *True* or *False*?

QUIZ

1 All fish live near the surface of the water.
2 Some fish never see daylight.
3 Saltwater fish always live in the sea.
4 Some fish can live in salt water and fresh water.

3 Listen, read and check your answers. 2.24

Fish live in water. Fish live in seas, rivers and lakes.

Different fish live in very different places. Small fish need hiding places to escape from bigger fish.

Some fish live near the surface. Some fish live on the bottom. Some fish live at the bottom of the deepest oceans and never see daylight! These fish have big mouths, like the anglerfish. Some fish make their own light, like the lanternfish.

The quantity of salt in the water is very important. Most lakes and rivers are fresh water. Fresh water has much less salt than the ocean. Most freshwater fish cannot live in salt water. Pike and trout are freshwater fish.

Most saltwater fish cannot live in fresh water. Cod and sardines are saltwater fish. They live in the sea.

Some fish can live in both fresh and salt water. Salmon live in salt water, but swim up rivers to lay their eggs. Eels live in fresh water but swim to the sea to lay their eggs.

1 Listen and find. 🎧 2.25

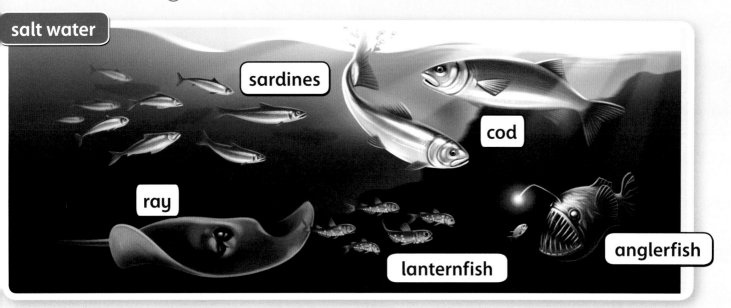

salt water

sardines

cod

ray

lanternfish

anglerfish

fresh water

trout

pike

2 Ask and answer.

What's this fish?

It's a ray. It lives in salt water. It lives near the bottom

Talk about it!

It's a ray.

It lives in salt water.

It lives near the bottom.

sardine cod trout
anglerfish pike
lanternfish

fresh water

near the surface
in the deepest oceans

1 Make fish tanks.

1 Draw.

2 Colour.

3 Write.

1 Listen, find and repeat. 2.26   **2 Listen and say the chant.** 2.27   Chant

aʊ
mouse

eɪ
snake

eə
stairs

Did you go to the old dark house?
Yes, we did, we saw a mouse.
We saw a spider, we saw a snake.
It was very big, it made me shake!

Were you frightened, were you scared?
Yes, we were, we ran downstairs.

6 The new computer

1 **Look, listen and repeat.** 🔊 2.28
2 **Listen and find.** 🔊 2.29

1 TV   2 radio   3 laptop   4 mouse   5 screen   6 keyboard
7 computer   8 camera   9 memory stick   10 text message   11 mobile phone

3 **Ask and answer.**

Does she need a mouse?

Yes, she does.

Does she need a radio?

No, she doesn't.

1 Listen and read. 🎵 2.31

We saved the club!

1 A reporter arrives at the club.

So tell us — what happened yesterday?

2 The children tell the story.

Well, we had a great day. There was a football match.

Oops — missed!

3 Then there were some fireworks, but Coco was scared and went into the club.

4 But a burglar opened the window and climbed in. He wanted the new computer.

Did you see the burglar?

5 No, the fireworks were very loud — we didn't see or hear anything.

Oh good. The computer is new.

6 The burglar tried to take the computer. But then he fell over Coco ...

CRASH!

Oh no!

2 **Look at the story and correct one word.**

reporter

1 A ~~footballer~~ arrives at the club.
2 There was a basketball match.
3 Molly went into the club.
4 A burglar opened the door.
5 He wanted to take the new phone.
6 The children chased the reporter.
7 The children saved the burglar!

3 **Answer and write _Yes_ or _No_.**

1 Did the children play football?
2 Did Archie get a goal?
3 Did Coco like the fireworks?
4 Did Coco chase the burglar?
5 Did the burglar fall into the goal?
6 Did the children stop the burglar?

4 **Listen again and act.** 2.31

1 Which sentence is in the story? Make more sentences.

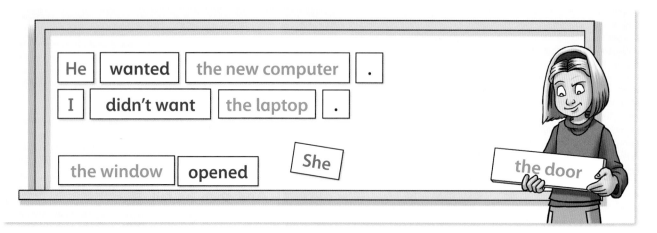

He | wanted | the new computer | .

I | didn't want | the laptop | .

the window | opened | She | the door

2 Listen and say which house. 2.32

3 Play the game.

He didn't open the window. He opened the door.

OK.

He didn't want the mobile phone. He wanted the television.

I know. Number 85!

That's right!

4 Write *True* or *False*. Then write four true or false sentences for your partner.

1 He wanted the television from number 48.

2 He didn't want the mobile phone from number 62.

3 He wanted the laptop from number 91.

4 He didn't want the television from number 85.

1 Look and read quickly. Match the photos to the posts.

Football match

(posted on Monday 12th May by Alex)

I played in a football match after school. We won the match! The score was 3–1. I scored the third goal. Fantastic!

It was a sunny day. After the match, we had a <u>barbecue</u> at school. Mr Jenkins cooked the food. I had a burger and some salad.

Rain!

(posted on Sunday 11th May by Alex)

It rained again today! I stayed at home in the morning and played computer games. I've got a new game called '<u>Pirate Ship</u>'. It's brilliant. You look for <u>treasure</u> and put it in your ship.

In the afternoon, I went to the new swimming pool with my mum and my sister. I played on the slide for an hour.

Day with Sam

(posted on Saturday 10th May by Alex)

I went to Sam's house today. Before lunch, we went rollerblading in the park. I'm not very good at rollerblading, but I'm learning. At half past twelve it started to rain, so we went back to Sam's house and had lunch.

We played <u>chess</u> in the afternoon. I'm quite good at chess, but Sam won!

2 Read the blog again and answer.

1 Who scored the third goal?

2 What was the weather like on Monday?

3 What did Alex eat at the barbecue?

4 When did Alex go swimming?

5 Who went swimming with him?

6 What was the weather like on Sunday?

7 Where did Alex go rollerblading?

8 Who won the chess game?

3 Find these words in the text.

Sending messages

1 Look, listen and repeat. 🎧 2.36

Messages you can see

mirror

smoke

flags

Messages you can hear

Morse code

drums

Messages using animals

horse

pigeon

2 Answer the questions.

1 How do you communicate?

   a by phone   **b** by text message   **c** by email   **d** by letter

2 What's your favourite way of sending a message?

1 Listen, read and answer. 2.37

2 Listen and find. 2.38

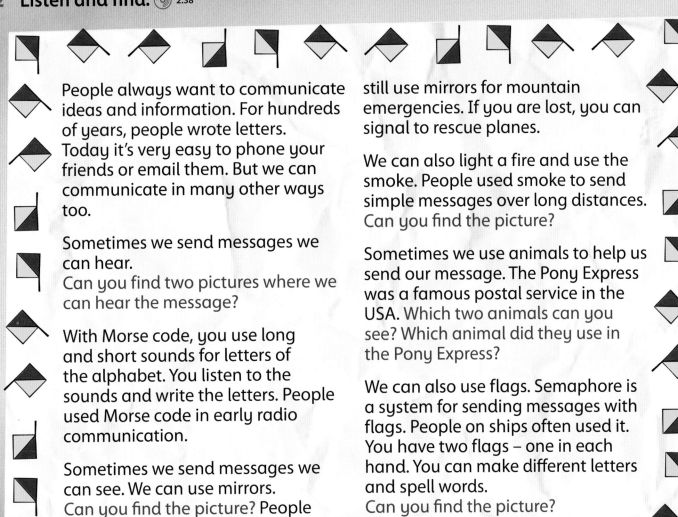

People always want to communicate ideas and information. For hundreds of years, people wrote letters.
Today it's very easy to phone your friends or email them. But we can communicate in many other ways too.

Sometimes we send messages we can hear.
Can you find two pictures where we can hear the message?

With Morse code, you use long and short sounds for letters of the alphabet. You listen to the sounds and write the letters. People used Morse code in early radio communication.

Sometimes we send messages we can see. We can use mirrors.
Can you find the picture? People still use mirrors for mountain emergencies. If you are lost, you can signal to rescue planes.

We can also light a fire and use the smoke. People used smoke to send simple messages over long distances.
Can you find the picture?

Sometimes we use animals to help us send our message. The Pony Express was a famous postal service in the USA. Which two animals can you see? Which animal did they use in the Pony Express?

We can also use flags. Semaphore is a system for sending messages with flags. People on ships often used it. You have two flags – one in each hand. You can make different letters and spell words.
Can you find the picture?

3 Mime and guess.

Are you sending a message with drums?

Yes, I am.

No, I'm not.

Talk about it!

Are you sending a message with   flags?
Morse code?
smoke?
mirrors?
drums?

1 Make a message.

1 Write a message.

2 Draw.

3 Play.

1 Listen, find and repeat. 🔊 2.39   2 Listen and say the chant. 🔊 2.40   Chant

 t danc**ed**

 d play**ed**

 **ɪd** want**ed**

I start**ed** my computer,
I play**ed** my favourite game.
The monkey jump**ed** from tree to tree,
It always did the same.

But then my screen explod**ed**,
The monkey jump**ed** right out!
He danc**ed** and wriggl**ed**,
He laugh**ed** and giggl**ed**,
He bounc**ed** and skipp**ed** about!

I turn**ed** off my computer,
I never play**ed** again!

Me and my world

1 **Look. Guess which text these words are in. Read and check.**

1 fish **2** camera **3** travel **4** swimming pool **6** scared **7** monkey

Jacques Cousteau is one of my heroes. This is my project about him.

medal

My hero is Tom Daley. I think he's brilliant. This is my project about him.

Jacques Cousteau was an underwater explorer, inventor and film director. He was born in France in 1910. He learned to swim when he was four.

In 1936 he used underwater goggles for the first time and saw hundreds of fish. He was amazed. He invented an underwater camera. This was the start of his career as a film director. Cousteau had a boat, called the Calypso. He travelled all over the world in the Calypso, making films and teaching people about the sea.

By Pierre, 9

Tom Daley is an Olympic diver. He was born in England in 1994. He started diving when he was eight. At the swimming pool, he watched people diving and he wanted to dive too. At first he was very scared, but then he discovered he loved diving.

He trains every day and he travels all over the world to competitions. He wins lots of medals. What's his secret? His lucky monkey toy. It always travels with him!

By Jackie, 10

scuba-diver

goggles

diver

2 **Read again and answer the questions.**

1 Where was Jacques Cousteau born?

2 Did he like the sea when he was a boy?

3 What did he invent?

4 Did he make films?

5 How old was Tom when he started diving?

6 Did he like diving at first?

7 Why does he travel?

8 Does he travel with his teddy?

Revision

Play the game!

 Say

 Ask and answer

 Sing a song

W Say a word beginning with these letters

Talk about it

1 Play in pairs. You need 3 counters each.

2 Put your counter on a square and follow the instructions.

3 Take turns.

4 Make a line of 3 to win!

Daniel Jones
History 2/10
Maths 9/10
Geography 5/10

W p m g

W s d b

Aquaworld ✓ ✗

W s m t

Learning to learn - Finding past forms

Swim-swimmed??
stop-stap??

1 Find the infinitive in your dictionary.

swim
(swam)

2 Find and underline the past form.

stop (stopping, stopped)
swim (swimming, swam, swum)

3 Can you find the past forms of these verbs?

drink   eat   learn   write   talk   want   wear

7 On the farm

1 Look, listen and repeat. 🔊 2.42
2 Listen and find. 🔊 2.43

1 grass   2 water   3 goat   4 weeds   5 peppers   6 tomatoes   7 onions
8 strawberries   9 cauliflower   10 milk   11 beans   12 potatoes

3 Ask and answer.

water   talk
eat   drink

What's Molly doing?

She's watering the peppers.

1 Listen and read. 2.45

Helping on the farm

1 The children are helping at their friend's farm.

Finn, can you get some water, please? Then you can all pick the beans. They're over there.

OK, Eve. Come on, Molly.

2 Where can I get some water, Eve?

There are some buckets and a tap over there. Thanks, kids, you're a great help.

3 Coco – you're not helping. Go away!

4 Coco! GO AWAY!

Watch out, Finn! Now my T-shirt is wet.

Oops! Sorry!

5 I like picking beans.

Me too!

6 OK, now let's water the tomatoes.

There's some water over there.

Oh no! The goat! Look! It's eating the plants!

7 Good work, kids. What's the matter?

Nothing!

8 Ouch. That hurts!

Sorry, Eve. The goat's eating the plants. We can't stop him!

9 It's OK – they're weeds!

So we are a great help!

And so is the goat!

2 Complete the summary.

Eve and the children are helping at their friend's ¹ __. Eve asks Finn to get some ² __ . Then the children pick the ³ __ and water the ⁴ __. Eve says they are a great help. Then a ⁵ __ eats some plants. Luke says sorry to Eve, but she isn't cross. The plants were ⁶ __ !

3 Answer. Write one or two words.

1 Who asks Finn to get some water?
2 Who says thank you to the children?
3 Who is cross with Coco?
4 Who's got a wet T-shirt?
5 Who picks beans with Finn and Archie?
6 Who eats the plants?

4 Listen again and act. 🔊 2.45

1   Which sentence is in the story? Make more sentences.

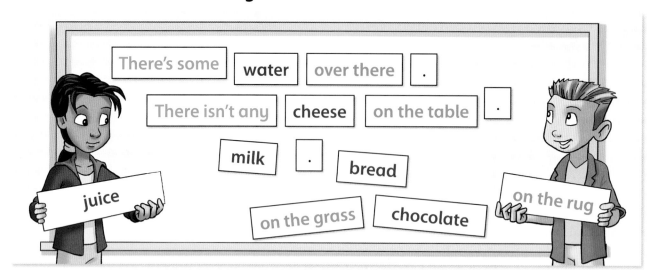

2   Look at the picture. Then cover it, listen and say *True* or *False*. 2.46

3   Cover the picture and play the game.

4   Write *True* or *False*. Then write four true or false sentences for your partner.

1   There's some water on the table.

2   There isn't any cheese on the grass.

3   There's some chocolate on the rug.

4   There isn't any bread on the table.

1 Look and read quickly. Which of these activities are mentioned?

1 going to the beach 2 playing tennis 3 working on a farm 4 swimming

AN UNUSUAL HOLIDAY

Meet Mike and Kerry Benson, and their children Emily and Jim. They usually go to the beach in the summer, but this year they wanted to do something different. One day they saw a TV programme about working holidays. Kerry said, "Mike was very excited because he's bored of beach holidays." They found some information on the internet and they decided to go on a working holiday in Spain.

They went to a farm in the <u>mountains</u>, in the south of Spain. The farmer grows <u>olives</u>, and he grows

vegetables too. It is hard work so he needs people to help him. "The Benson family picked the olives for me," he said. "It isn't an easy job!"

The family stayed in a <u>cottage</u>. It didn't have electricity or water, so they got their water from a <u>tap</u> outside the cottage. They worked hard, but they had fun too. There was a small swimming pool, so they swam every evening. On Saturdays and Sundays, they visited towns and beaches. "We saw some interesting places," said Emily. "But the best part of the holiday was being on the farm!"

2 Read the article again and answer.

1 How many children have Mike and Kerry got?
2 Where do they usually go in the summer?
3 Which country did they go to this year?
4 What does the farmer grow?
5 How did the Bensons help him?
6 How often did they swim in the pool?
7 What did they do at the weekends?
8 Did Emily like the farm?

3 Find these words in the text.

How plants grow

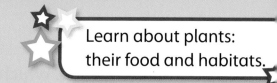

1 Look and read.

2 Listen, read and answer. 2.50

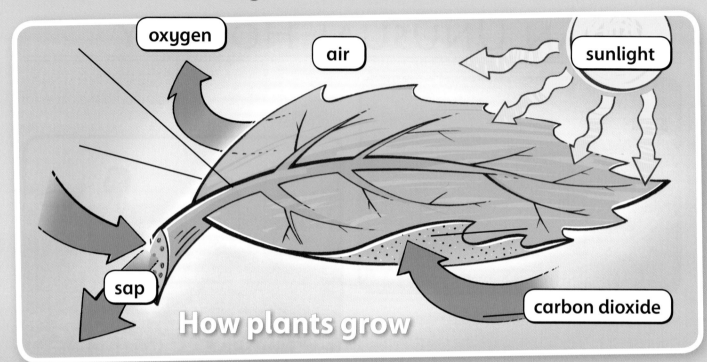

oxygen

air

sunlight

sap

carbon dioxide

How plants grow

There are thousands of different types of plants. Some grow in hot, dry deserts. Can you think of a plant that grows in the desert?

Some plants grow in cold, wet forests. Some grow under the ice and snow! Do you know any plants that grow in cold places?

Plants can make their own food. This process is called photosynthesis. They need air, water and sunlight. The plants take a gas called carbon dioxide from the air and water from the rain. Then they use the sunlight to produce oxygen. The oxygen goes back into the air. The plants change the carbon dioxide and water into food. This food is very sugary. It is called sap. This all happens in the leaves of the plant. The sap then travels from the leaves into the stem. Then it can go to where the plant needs food.

3 Read and write *True* or *False*.

1 Plants can grow when it is hot.

2 Plants can't grow when it is very cold.

3 Plants need sunlight to make food.

4 Sap is sugary.

5 The sap begins in the stems.

1 **Look, listen and repeat.** 2.51 **2** **Look, listen and find.** 2.52

sunflowers

hot

sunny

pine trees

needles

wet

cold

dry

cacti

spikes

palm tree

leaves

ferns

shady

3 **Ask and answer.**

Tell me about sunflowers.

They grow in hot, sunny places. They've got big, yellow flowers.

Talk about it!

They grow in hot, sunny places. | wet shady
cold dry

They've got big, yellow flowers. | leaves spikes
needles

1 Make a plant table.

1 Draw and colour.   2 Tick.   3 Write.

1 Listen, find and repeat. 🎧 2.53   **2 Listen and say the chant.** 🎧 2.54   **Chant**

əʊ   goat

æ   cat

40 goats,
50 cats,
60 coats,
70 hats,
80 boats,
90 rats,
And one hundred acrobats!

8 Favourite animals

1 **Look, listen and repeat.** 🔊 3.1
2 **Listen and find.** 🔊 3.2

Our favourite animals

1 spider   2 elephant   3 kangaroo   4 polar bear   5 panda   6 camel
7 tortoise   8 swan   9 bee   10 frog   11 hippo   12 mouse

3 **Ask and answer.**

It's white and it's got wings. It can fly. What is it?

It's a swan.

1 Listen and read. 3.4

The new cat

1 At the club ...

Look at our biscuits! There are mice everywhere!

Look at my crisps! Get the mice, Coco!

2 We need a faster cat. This is Billy. He's faster than Coco.

Billy's bigger than Coco too. Catch the mice, Billy!

3 Oh dear. Billy's in Coco's bed. Poor Coco!

Coco's smaller than Billy, but I think she's nicer!

4 One, two, three, four ... That's five mice now.

Well done, Billy! You're the best!

5 Poor Coco. You don't like the new cat.

I don't like him either. We should help Coco.

6 Look, there's the last mouse! Go, Billy!

Come on, Coco, you can do it.

7 Go on, Coco!

2 Read and match.

1	Billy is bigger and faster	a Billy.
2	Coco doesn't like	b the last mouse.
3	Molly thinks	c than Coco.
4	Coco catches	d Coco is the best.

3 Answer. Write one word.

1 What's the new cat's name? _____

2 Who thinks Coco is nicer than the new cat? _____

3 How many mice does Billy catch? _____

4 Who says Billy is the best? _____

5 How many mice does Coco catch? _____

6 Who catches the last mouse? _____

4 Listen again and act. 3.4

1   Which sentence is in the story? Make more sentences.

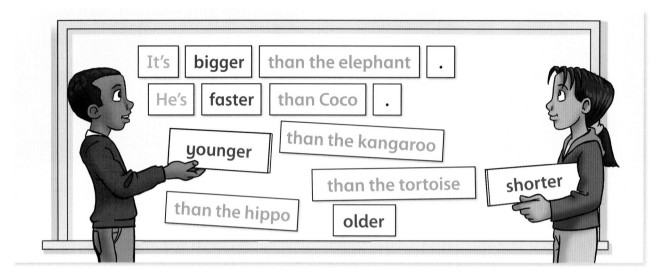

It's **bigger** than the elephant .

He's **faster** than Coco .

younger   than the kangaroo

than the tortoise   **shorter**

than the hippo   **older**

2   Listen and say which animal. 🎧 3.5

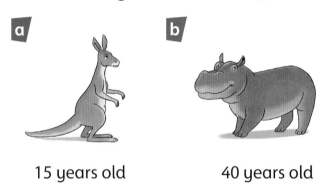

a   **b**

15 years old   40 years old

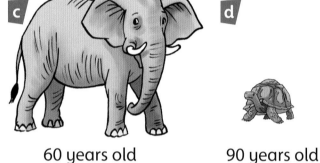

c   **d**

60 years old   90 years old

3   Play the game.

It's older than the hippo.

Go on.

And it's shorter than the elephant.

I know! The tortoise!

That's right!

4   Complete. Then write four sentences for your partner to complete. 🖊

1   The hippo is taller than the _____ .

2   The elephant is older than the _____ and the _____ .

3   The kangaroo is shorter than the _____ .

4   The hippo is younger than the _____ and the _____ .

1 Match the words to the pictures.

1 fur

2 whale

3 mouth

4 skin

 **a**

 **b**

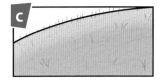 **c**

 **d**

2 Do the quiz. Then check your answers.

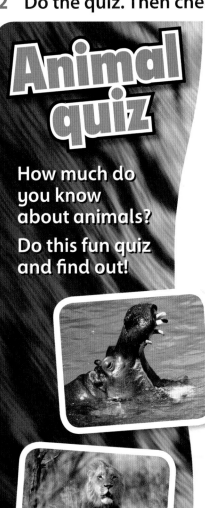

Animal quiz

How much do you know about animals?

Do this fun quiz and find out!

1 How many legs has a spider got?

a Six.
b Eight.
c It hasn't got any legs.

2 What do hippos eat?

a Plants.
b Fish.
c Plants and fish.

3 How does a frog drink water?

a Through its skin.
b Through its mouth.
c Frogs don't need to drink water.

4 What is the largest animal in the world?

a The African elephant.
b The blue whale.
c The hippo.

5 How long is a lion's tail?

a 2 metres.
b nearly 1 metre.
c 30 centimetres.

6 Which animal can live without water for nearly a month?

a A swan.
b An elephant.
c A camel.

7 What colour are a polar bear's fur and skin?

a Its fur is purple but its skin is green.
b Its fur is white but its skin is black.
c Its fur and skin are white.

8 How tall is a giraffe?

a Five metres.
b Ten metres.
c One metre.

9 Where do pandas live?

a In China.
b In India and China.
c In South America.

10 How many teeth has a crocodile got?

a Twelve.
b Between 20 and 40.
c Between 64 and 70.

Answers:
1b 2a 3a 4b 5a 6c 7b 8a 9a 10c

3 Complete the sentences.

1 A camel can live without _____ for several weeks.

2 A spider has got _____ .

3 Hippos eat _____ .

4 The _____ is bigger than the African elephant .

Bees

1 Look, listen and repeat. 3.9

2 Listen, read and answer. 3.10

beehive

worker

comb

honey

queen

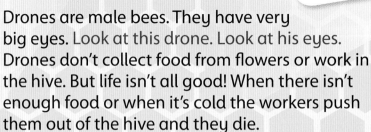

drone

Honey bees are social insects. There are different types of bees – drones, workers and queen bees. They live together in a beehive.

The work in a beehive is divided beween the bees. The queen is the biggest bee in the colony. She is the only bee that lays eggs. Sometimes a queen can lay **3,000** eggs in a single day. Can you find the queen in this picture?

Worker bees are female, but do not lay eggs. A colony can have **50,000** to **60,000** workers. Workers give food to the queen and babies. They clean the hive. Some workers build the comb and store the food. Older workers collect the food from the flowers and make the honey. What is the worker bee doing in this picture?

People collect the combs from the beehive. They put the honey in jars and we eat it – yum! Can you see the comb in this jar?

Drones are male bees. They have very big eyes. Look at this drone. Look at his eyes. Drones don't collect food from flowers or work in the hive. But life isn't all good! When there isn't enough food or when it's cold the workers push them out of the hive and they die.

3 Read and answer.

Queen, drone or worker?

1 This bee lays eggs.

2 This bee cleans the hive.

3 This bee collects the food.

4 This bee doesn't work.

5 This bee makes honey.

6 This bee is bigger than the others.

1 Listen and find. 🎧 3.11

2 Talk about the bees.

Tell me about this bee.

It's female. It lays eggs. It's the queen.

Talk about it!

It's female.   male

It collects food.   gives food to the queen
cleans the hive   doesn't work very hard
makes the comb   makes honey
lays eggs   has got big eyes

It's a worker.   the queen   a drone

1 Make a bee diagram.

1 Draw and colour.

2 Write.

1 Listen, find and repeat. 3.12   **2 Listen and say the chant.** 3.13

ə

faster

I'm bigger than my sister,
But smaller than my mum.
I'm faster than my brother,
Especially when we run!

I'm stronger than my cousin,
But weaker than my dad.
I'm faster than my brother,
Especially when I'm bad!

9 / At the bike track

1 **Look, listen and repeat.** 🔊 3.14
2 **Listen and find.** 🔊 3.15

1 traffic lights **2** car **3** sign **4** stop **5** bike **6** zebra crossing
7 road **8** helmet **9** gloves **10** go left **11** go right

3 Ask and answer.

> Start at B.
> How do you get to D?

> Go left past the bike. Go right.
> Go over the zebra crossing and
> go through the traffic lights.

1 Listen and read. 🔊 3.18

2 Complete the summary.

The children are in the ¹ _____.
Luke wants everyone to be ² __.
He tells them to wear a ³ __ and he
tells them some ⁴ __. Suddenly his bike
slips. He goes into the ⁵ __ , and finally
he falls into a ⁶ __. Everyone laughs!

3 Look at the story and correct one word.

1 Jazmin loves cycling ~~up~~ *down* hills.

2 Luke tells everyone to start.

3 Luke says you must wear a jacket.

4 Luke wants to tell everyone some stories.

5 Luke falls into a tree.

4 Listen again and act. 🎧 3.18

1   Which sentence is in the story? Make more sentences.

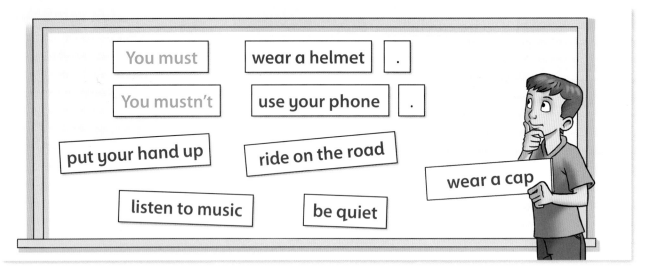

You must | wear a helmet   .

You mustn't | use your phone   .

put your hand up   ride on the road   wear a cap

listen to music   be quiet

2   Listen and say where they are. 3.19

on bikes

in class

in the library

on skateboards

at the swimming pool

3   Play the game.

We must wear a helmet.

Alright.

And we mustn't ride on the path.

I know! We're on bikes.

4   Complete. Then write three sentences for your partner to complete.

1   When you're ___ , you mustn't listen to music and you must wear a cap.

2   When you're ___ , you must wear a helmet and you mustn't ride on the road.

1 Look and read quickly. Match the headings to the paragraphs.

Safety General information Bike tracks

Welcome to Middleton Woods!

1

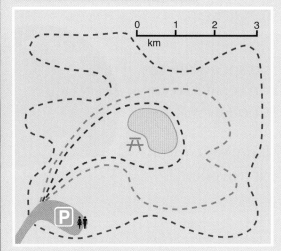

Red track: 10 km, difficult. This track is for off-road bikes only.

Blue track: 6 km, not too difficult. This track is for all types of bike, but you need to be <u>fit</u>. You need to cycle up and down hills, so check your <u>brakes</u> before you start!

Purple track: 4 km, easy. This track is for everyone. It is suitable for families and young children.

2

Remember these simple rules, to keep you and other people safe:

1 Always wear a helmet when you cycle.

2 Stay on the correct track – follow the <u>arrows</u> on the signs.

3 Children under 12 must cycle with an adult.

4 Don't forget to carry water bottles when the weather is hot.

3

 Car park opening times:

1st May–30th Sept	8.30am–6.30pm
1st Oct–30th April	10.00am–5.00pm
The car park is closed on Mondays.	

 The toilets are next to the car park.

 There is a picnic area on the blue track, near the <u>pond</u>. Please put your rubbish in the bins when you leave.

No fires!

2 Read the sign again and write *True* or *False*.

1 There are some hills on the blue track.

2 The red track is easy.

3 The purple track is easier than the blue track.

4 Children can use the purple track.

5 If you are nine, you must cycle with an adult.

6 You can park your car at 9.00am on 15th June.

7 The toilets are next to the pond.

3 Find these words in the text.

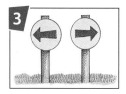

Speed

1   Listen, read and answer. 3.23

How do you go to school each day? Do you walk? Do you ride your bike or go by bus? Do you go by car? How far do you travel? How long does it take?

We measure speed in kilometres per hour. In many towns in Europe, the speed limit is **50** kilometres per hour (km/h). On many motorways the speed limit is **120** kilometres per hour.

Road signs show the speed limit. How fast can you travel if you see this sign?

This is a speedometer. You can see it in a car. It tells you how fast the car is travelling. How fast is this car travelling?

This is the fastest car in the world. It can travel at **1,228** kilometres per hour!

To calculate speed, we use the distance-speed-time triangle.

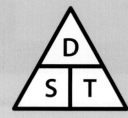

D = distance
S = speed
T = time

To calculate speed, you divide distance by time. For example, a car travels **80km** in **2 hours**. $\frac{80}{2}$ = **40**. So the car is travelling at **40** kilometres per hour (**40 km/h**).

2   Read and answer.

1   What's the speed limit in many towns in Europe?

2   What's the speed limit on many motorways?

3   How fast can the fastest car travel?

4   How do we calculate speed?

1 Listen and match. 3.24

1 person

2 car

3 cheetah

4 racing car

5 plane

6 space shuttle

1	A person can walk at about	a	1000 km/h
2	A car in town can travel at	b	6 km/h
3	A cheetah can run at	c	360 km/h
4	A racing car can travel at	d	100 km/h
5	A plane can travel at	e	50 km/h
6	A space shuttle can travel at	f	26,000 km/h

2 Ask and answer

 Talk about it!

How fast can a racing car travel?

360 kilometres per hour.

How fast can	a racing car	travel?
	a car in town	
	a plane	
	a space shuttle	
	a person	walk?
	a cheetah	run?

1 Make a scale.

1 Draw and colour. 2 Write.

1 Listen, find and repeat. 3.26   **2 Listen and say the chant.** 3.27   Chant

cake

cycling

There's a circus in the city.
In the circus, there's a clown.
He likes cakes and he likes cycling,
And he wears a funny crown!

He's a clown,
A cycling clown,
He eats cakes and wears a crown!

He's a clown,
A cycling clown,
He's a crazy, cycling clown!

Me and my world

1 Look. Guess which text these words are in. Read and check.

| 1 / purple | 2 / autumn | 3 / tree | 4 / leaf | 5 / flower | 6 / flag |

bulbs

Hi, my name's Anya. I live on a tulip farm, in Holland. Tulips are Holland's national flower. There are about 3 billion tulips in Holland. That's 3,000,000,000,000. That's a lot of tulips!

Tulips can be many different colours. But the most famous tulip is the Queen of the Night. It looks black, but in fact it's very dark purple.

We plant the tulips in October and November. They flower in May. Lots of people visit the fields because they are very beautiful. Did you know? You can eat tulip bulbs – and the flowers too!

My name is Matt and I'm from Canada. We've got a national tree, the maple tree. It has beautiful red and yellow leaves in the autumn. There is a maple leaf on the Canadian flag, and on one of our coins too. Our favourite breakfast is pancakes with maple syrup!

Maple syrup is made from maple sap. Many maple trees have a tap with a bucket under it. In the spring the sap flows out of the tree into the bucket. One tree produces about 40 litres of sap, and this makes about 1 litre of syrup.

sap

maple syrup

2 Read again and answer the questions.

1 Where does Anya live?

2 How many tulips are there in Holland?

3 What colour is the Queen of the Night?

4 What parts of the tulip can you eat?

5 What is the Canadian national tree?

6 Where can you see the maple leaf?

7 What do Canadians eat with their pancakes?

8 When does the sap flow from the maple trees?

 Say

 Ask and answer

Sing a song

W Say a word beginning with these letters

Talk about it

1 Play in pairs. You need 3 counters each.

2 Put your counter on a square and follow the instructions.

3 Take turns.

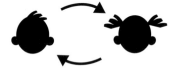

4 Make a line of 3 to win!

Learning to learn - Checking spelling

thin (thinner, thinnest)

tooth (teeth)

1 Find the adjective. Look at the superlative form.

2 Find the singular word. Look at the plural form.

3 Check the spellings of these words. Are they correct?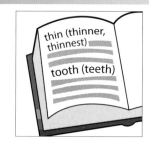

dry – dryer   tooth – tooths   new – newwer   child – childs

thin - thinner   beach - beaches

World Car Free Day

1 **Look, listen and repeat.** 🎧 3.29 **Look and find.**

tandem   tram   bus   clean   dirty

2 **Who made the posters? Read and match.**

We are doing a project about World Car Free Day. On this day many people don't use their cars. They go by bus. They ride their bikes. They walk. It's a great idea. Here are our posters.

There's a tandem on my poster. There are flowers and trees too. They are happy because the air is clean.

My poster is a picture of a city. There are lots and lots of cars. They are noisy and dirty. There's a man in the middle. He can't escape!

We can travel in lots of different ways. You can see a bus and a tram and on my poster. There's a bike with a trailer for children or shopping bags. Look, there are children in a walking bus too!

3 **Listen and answer for Finn, Jazmin and Archie.** 🎧 3.30

1 What is he / she doing on World Car Free Day?

2 Who is he / she with?

3 Where is he / she going?

4 Why?

Pancake Day

1 **Look, listen and repeat.** 🎧 3.31

2 **Look and find.**

nuts   chocolate sauce   syrup   sugar   lemon   honey   jam   strawberries

3 **Listen and find.** 🎧 3.32

4 **Read and match.** ✏️

a Do you like my pancake? It's got chocolate sauce and nuts.

b My pancake is lovely. I don't like lots of sweet things so it's only got lemon, strawberries and a little sugar.

c Mmm! I like syrup. My pancake's got syrup and nuts. It hasn't got any chocolate.

d I like all of the toppings. But on my pancake I've got my favourite – jam.

World Book Day

1 **Look, listen and repeat.** 🎧 3.33

2 **Listen and find.** 🎧 3.34

adventure   comic   story   heroes   superheroes   mystery   fairy tale

3 **Read and match.** ✏️

a

I like fairy tales and adventures.
I don't like mystery books.

b

I like comics about superheroes and I also like adventures. I don't like fairy tales at all!

c

I love story books about girls and I like mystery books. I never read comics.

d

I like true stories about sports heroes.
I don't like mystery books.

4 **Ask and answer.**

What's your favourite book?

It's called Incredible Man.

What's it about?

It's about a superhero. He is very strong and he helps people.

1 Read. Circle the correct word.

1 Giraffes live (in) / at Africa.

2 They **has** / **have** got very long necks.

3 **Her** / **Their** legs are very long too.

4 **Every** / **All** giraffes can run fast.

5 A giraffe **doesn't** / **don't** eat meat.

6 It eats leaves **from** / **to** trees.

7 **Lots** / **Many** of people like looking at giraffes.

8 You can **seeing** / **see** giraffes at the zoo.

2 Read. Choose the right word and write them on the lines.

Lots of children like __playing__ football. You can play at school or you can play

1 _____ the park. Football players

2 _____ shorts and football boots.

Football matches are often 3 _____

Saturday afternoons. If 4 _____ want

to play football, you can 5 _____ to a

sports centre.

Example	play	(playing)	played
1	in	on	to
2	wearing	wear	do
3	at	in	on
4	she	your	you
5	find	go	play

 **Reading & Writing**

Read the text. Choose the right words and write them on the lines.

Supermarkets

Example   Where ____do____ you buy your food? Most people go to a

1   market _____ a supermarket. You can usually buy all

the food you need in a supermarket. Lots of supermarkets have

2   other things _____ , like books, toys and clothes. Some

3   supermarkets _____ a café where you can buy a drink

or something to eat. You can park your car in the car park

4   _____ the supermarket. When you finish your shopping,

5   you can put your bags in the car _____ go home. It's easy!

Example	have	buy	do
1	or	to	so
2	some	and	too
3	having	have	got
4	outside	next	where
5	and	because	but

Let's practise!

1 Look, read and match.

You can eat this.

This is part of your body.

This animal can swim.

You can wear this.

You can use this to keep warm in bed.

This is for eating soup or cereal out of.

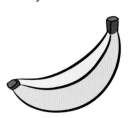

2 Read and correct one word.

| ~~sandwiches~~ neck teeth water reading wash |

1  **a scarf**   You wear this around your leg. _____

2  **a swimming pool**   It has got sand in it and children play in it.
_____

3  **a bathroom**   This is part of a house. You sleep there.
_____

4  **bread**   You use this to make ~~cakes~~. _sandwiches_

5 **comics**   Children like eating these. There are lots of
pictures in them. _____

6 **a toothbrush**   You use this to clean your shoes. _____

Reading & Writing

Look and read. Choose the correct words and write them on the lines. There is one example.

a hospital

a lizard

milk

a doctor

a dolphin

water

a parrot

a mountain

Example

This animal lives in the sea and it eats fish.   <u>a dolphin</u>

Questions

1 This is a white drink. It comes from cows.   _____

2 You stay here when you are ill. Nurses work here.   _____

3 This is very big. Sometimes you can see a long way if you
   climb to the top.   _____

4 It lives in hot countries and it has got four legs and a tail.   _____

5 You drink this when you are thirsty and you can find it in a river.   _____

6 This animal can fly. It has got coloured feathers.   _____

Movers Let's practise!

1 Look, read and match.

1 The girl who is writing on the board   **a** are next to the window.

2 The boy with red hair   **b** is wearing brown trousers.

3 The boys that are reading   **c** has got blond hair.

4 The one with glasses   **d** are sitting on blue chairs.

5 The girls who are making a plane   **e** has got some purple paint.

6 The one with blue shoes   **f** is reading a book about cars.

2 Look at the picture above and complete the sentences.

> who is drawing   with a red book   who are reading   ~~with brown hair~~
>
> with a green jumper   who are next to the board

1 The girl ____with brown hair____ is making a plane.

2 The children _____ are boys.

3 The girl _____ is writing.

4 The boy _____ has got a black pen.

5 The children _____ have got black trousers.

6 The boy _____ is wearing glasses.

Listening

Listen and draw lines. There is one example. 🎧 3.35

Ben   Daisy   Sam

Nick   Peter   Jill

 **Let's practise!**

1 Read and write *True* or *False*.

Max phoned his friend Joe, on Sunday morning. "Let's go to the park this afternoon," he said. But Joe didn't want to. They decided to go a wood. First Max went to Joe's hou and they made a picnic. They made some sandwiches and Joe's mum helped them. She gave them some biscuits and apples. Then they cycled to the woods. They ate their picnic under a tree. After lunch, they climbed a big tree.

1 Max has got a friend who is called Joe. ___True.___

2 Max phoned Joe on Sunday afternoon. _____

3 Max didn't want to go to the park. _____

4 The boys made a picnic at Joe's house. _____

5 Joe's mum helped Max and Joe to make a cake. _____

6 The boys climbed a tree and then they had their picnic.

_____

2 Read and complete the sentences. Use 1, 2 or 3 words.

1 Ann gave John a cake, but he didn't like it.

➔ John didn't enjoy ___the cake___ .

2 Lucy and Tom went to the beach. They played in the sea.

➔ _____ played in the water.

3 Jack watched a film about a dinosaur. It was very scary.

➔ _____ in the film was scary.

4 "My friends are in the park," said May. "I want to play with them!"

➔ May wanted to play with _____.

5 Alex wanted to eat pizza on his birthday. Sally and Fred went to a restaurant with him.

➔ Sally and Fred went to a pizza restaurant with _____ .

Look at the pictures and read the story. Write some words to complete the sentences about the story. You can use 1, 2 or 3 words.

The birthday surprise

Sam is ten years old. Last Saturday morning he was very excited because it was his birthday. He went into the kitchen at half past eight. His mum was there. She smiled but she didn't say "Happy birthday". Sam was sad. He went outside to play on his skateboard. But he crashed into the wall. "Oh no," he shouted. "It's broken!"

Example

It was Sam's __birthday__ last Saturday.

Questions

1 His mum was _____ at half past eight.

2 Sam _____ because his mum didn't say "Happy birthday".

3 Sam crashed _____ .

At ten o'clock, Sam's mum shouted, "Sam, come inside, please." Sam slowly walked into the house. Then he heard people talking. He went into the living room. All of his friends were there and they had a birthday cake for him! They shouted "Surprise!" and Sam smiled. His mum and dad gave him a big present. He opened it; it was a new skateboard!

4 At ten o'clock, Sam's mum asked him to _____ .

5 Sam heard _____ in the house.

6 His friends had _____ for Sam.

7 The big present was _____ .

Syllabus

Unit	Structures	Vocabulary	'Learning through English' topic and language	Writing
1	**Collocations with *go/play*** go climbing / rollerblading / fishing / rowing / sailing / skateboarding / swimming / water skiing play tennis / football / basketball / hide and seek / **Present Simple (*want to* + verb)** I want to (play basketball). I don't want to (go swimming). ***Let's* + verb** Let's (go sailing). ***can* (for ability)** Can you (swim)? Yes, I can. / No, I can't. ***You can…* (for possibility)** You can (go swimming) on Monday.	**Outdoor activities** climb, fish, play basketball, play football, play hide and seek, play tennis, rollerblade, row, sail, skateboard, swim, waterski	*Geography: The water cycle and the weather* **Weather** sunny, cloudy, windy, raining, snowing, foggy, stormy, (10) degrees, minus (5)	**Writing task:** An email **Writing tip:** Adverbs of frequency
2	**Present Simple (for daily routine)** She gets up (at six o'clock). I go to bed (at eight o'clock). We have dinner (at seven o'clock) What time do you get up? What time does he get up? **Prepositions** Where's (Finn)? He's behind (the doctor). behind / next to / in front of / under / on	**Jobs** actor, artist, astronaut, dancer, doctor, firefighter, footballer, pilot, pirate, policeman, scientist, teacher	*Art: Draw with a grid* **Numbers and dates** one hundred five hundred and thirty-one one thousand 1975 2019	**Writing task:** An interview **Writing tip:** like, love + geru
3	***should*** You should (sit down). You shouldn't (eat sweets). **Object pronouns** Can (you) help me? I can help (you). us / them / him / her / you / me ***I've got* (+illnesses)** What's the matter? I've got (a headache).	**Health** I feel … dizzy / sick. I've got … a cold / a cough / an earache / a headache / a sore throat / a stomach ache / a toothache.	*Science: Pulse rates* **Hand and heart** blood, fingers, heart, thumb, wrist, pulse	**Writing task:** A poster **Writing tip:** Starting and en sentences and of commas
4	**Past simple (*was / wasn't*)** I was (good at History). She wasn't (good at Maths). **Past simple questions and short answers (*was / wasn't*)** Were you (good at History)? Was he (good at Science)? Were they (good at art)? Yes, I was. / No, he wasn't. / No, they weren't. **Questions with *Which*** Which do you prefer, (Maths or Music)?	**School** Art, English, Geography, History, Maths, Music, P.E., Science, Spanish, classroom, poster	*History: Ancient Egypt* **Ancient Egypt** god, goddess, headdress, mummy, pharaoh, pyramid	**Writing task:** A description **Writing tip:** Expressing quantities

Unit	Structures	Vocabulary	'Learning through English' topic and language	Writing
5	**Past simple (irregular verbs)** I saw (an octopus). He didn't see (a shark). **Past simple questions and short answers** Did you go (to the beach)? Yes, I did. No I didn't. **Questions about quantity** How many (fish are there)? There are lots of (fish).	**Sea life** boat, crab, dolphin, fish, jellyfish, octopus, sand, seahorse, shark, shell, starfish, water	*Science: Fish* **Aquatic life** bottom, deep, lake, river, sea, shallow, surface	**Writing task:** A leaflet **Writing tip:** Useful language for giving information
6	**Past simple (regular verbs)** He wanted (the computer). He didn't want (the phone). What did you do (on Tuesday)? What did they do (at five o'clock)? **Present simple** Does she need a mouse? Yes, she does. / No, she doesn't	**Electrical items** camera, computer, keyboard, laptop, memory stick, mobile phone, mouse, radio, screen, text message, TV	*History: Sending messages* **Messages** flags, horse, mirror, Morse code, pigeon, smoke, drums	**Writing task:** A blog post **Writing tip:** Time phrases
7	*some/any* There's some (water). There isn't any (cheese). There are some (tomatoes). There aren't any (beans). **Present continuous** What's (she) doing? She's (watering the tomatoes).	**Farming** beans, cauliflower, goat, grass, milk, onions, peppers, potatoes, strawberries, tomatoes, water, weeds	*Science: How plants grow* **Habitats** hot, sunny, dry, wet, cold, shady	**Writing task:** A magazine article **Writing tip:** Speech marks
8	**Comparatives** (Billy's) faster than (Coco). The elephant is bigger than the hippo. **Superlatives** (Billy's) the biggest. The lion is the hungriest. **Present simple** It's white. It can fly. It's got wings.	**Animals** elephant, frog, hippo, polar bear, kangaroo, panda, tortoise, camel, swan, mouse, bee, spider	*Science: Bees* **Bees** beehive, comb, honey, queen, worker, drone	**Writing task:** Quiz questions **Writing tip:** Question words and question phrases
9	*must / mustn't* You must (wear a helmet). You mustn't (cross the road). **Can (for permission)** Can I (go and play)? Can I (have a biscuit)? **Directions** Go left/right at (the stop sign). Stop at the (traffic lights).	**Road safety** bike, car, gloves, go left, go right, helmet, road, sign, stop, traffic lights, zebra crossing	*Maths: Speed* **Large numbers** one thousand three thousand, seven hundred twenty-five thousand	**Writing task:** An information sign **Writing tip:** An overview of the most common types of punctuation

Wordlist

Unit 1

Can I try it? /kən aɪ 'traɪ ɪt/
climb /klaɪm/
cloudy /'klaʊdi/
condensation /kɒndenˈseɪʃn/
countryside /'kʌntrisaɪd/
degrees /dɪˈgriːz/
evaporation /ɪˈvæpəˈreɪʃn/
fish /fɪʃ/
foggy /'fɒgi/
Great idea! /'greɪt aɪdɪə/
Here we go! /'hɪə wi: gəʊ/
I don't feel like…
    /aɪ dəʊnt 'fiːl laɪk …/
Let's go … /lets 'gəʊ …/
minus /'maɪnəs/
play basketball
    /pleɪ 'baːskɪtbɔːl/
play football /pleɪ 'fʊtbɔːl/
play hide and seek
    /pleɪ haɪd ən 'siːk/
play tennis /pleɪ 'tenɪs/
rain drops /'reɪn drɒps/
raining /'reɪnɪŋ/
rollerblade /'rəʊləbleɪd/
row /rəʊ/
sail /seɪl/
scooter /'skuːtə(r)/
Shh! /ʃ/
skateboard /'skeɪtbɔːd/
sky /skaɪ/
slide /slaɪd/
snowing /'snəʊɪŋ/
standing /'stændɪŋ/
stormy /'stɔːmi/
sunny /'sʌni/
swim /swɪm/
swing /swɪŋ/
Wake up! /weɪk 'ʌp/
warm (v) /wɔːm/
water cycle /'wɔːtə saɪkl/
waterski /'wɔːtəski:/
water vapour /'wɔːtə 'veɪpə/
weather /'weðə(r)/
What time is it?
    /wɒt 'taɪm ɪz ɪt/
What's the weather like?
    /wɒts ðə 'weðə laɪk/
windy /'wɪndi/

Unit 2

actor /'/
always /'ɔːlweɪz/
artist /'aːtɪst/
astronaut /'æstrənɔːt/
behind /bɪˈhaɪnd/
chief /tʃiːf/
clock /klɒk/
Come on! /'kʌm ɒn/
dancer /'daːnsə(r)/
doctor /'dɒktə(r)/
Don't worry! /dəʊnt 'wʌri/
firefighter /'faɪəfaɪtə(r)/
footballer /'fʊtbɔːlə(r)/
Good idea! /gʊd aɪdɪə/
grid /grɪd/
in front of /ɪn 'frʌnt əv/
It's … metres high.
    /ɪts … miːtəz 'haɪ/
It was built in …
    /ɪt wəz 'bɪlt ɪn …/
lift (n) /lɪft/
never /'nevə/
next to /'nekst tu/
on /ɒn/
pilot /'paɪlət/
pirate /'paɪrət/
policeman /pəˈliːsmən/
restaurant /'restrɒnt/
sailor /'seɪlə(r)/
scientist /'saɪəntɪst/
singer /'sɪŋə(r)/
soldier /'səʊldʒə(r)/
stairs /steəz/
teacher /'tiːtʃə(r)/
tower /'taʊə(r)/
under /'ʌndə/
usually /'juːʒuəli/
What a mess! /wɒt ə 'mes/

Unit 3

Are we nearly there?
    /aː wi nɪəli 'ðeə(r)/
beats per minute
    /biːts pə 'mɪnɪt/
blood /blʌd/
bright /braɪt/
cheesecake /'tʃiːzkeɪk/
chicken /'tʃɪkɪn/
cold /kəʊld/
cough /kɒf/
dish /dɪʃ/
dizzy /'dɪzi/
earache /'ɪəreɪk/
fingers /'fɪŋgəz/
fit /fɪt/
headache /'hedeɪk/
heart /haːt/
Hurrah! /həˈraː/
I can't wait! /aɪ kaːnt 'weɪt/
I don't feel well.
    /aɪ dəʊnt fiːl 'wel/
I feel … /aɪ fiːl …/
I've got … /aɪv gɒt …/

Unit 4 (third column)

measure /'meʒə(r)/
Oh dear. /əʊ 'dɪə(r)/
press (v) /pres/
pulse /pʌls/
pump (v) /pʌmp/
shoes /ʃuːz/
sick /sɪk/
sore throat /sɔː 'θrəʊt/
stomach ache /'stʌməkeɪk/
Take your pulse.
    /teɪk jɔː 'pʌls/
thumb /θʌm/
toothache /'tuːθeɪk/
What's the matter?
    /wɒts ðə 'mætə(r)/
wrist /rɪst/

Me and my world 1

desert /'dezəˈrt/
foggy /'fɒgi/
guide /gaɪd/
Iceland /'aɪslənd/
meerkat /'mɪəkæt/
ocean /'əʊʃn/
sand /sænd/
seeds /siːdz/
South Africa /saʊθ 'æfrɪkə/
volcano /vɒl'keɪnəʊ/

Unit 4

Art /aːt/
ancient /'eɪnʃnt/
bandages /'bændɪdʒɪz/
believe /bɪˈliːv/
break /breɪk/
calculator /'kælkjəleɪtə(r)/
classroom /'klaːsruːm/
dead /ded/
die /daɪ/
English /'ɪŋglɪʃ/
feathers /'feðəz/
Geography /'dʒɒgrəfi/
god /gɒd/
goddess /'gɒdes/
headdress /'heddres/
History /'hɪstri/
horns /hɔːnz/
lucky /'lʌki/
Maths /mæθs/
medal /'medl/
mummy /'mʌmi/
Music /'mjuːzɪk/
No matter what.
    /nəʊ mætə 'wɒt/
P.E. /piː 'iː/
pharaoh /'feərəʊ/
poster /'pəʊstə(r)/
pyramid /'pɪrəmɪd/
school lunches /skuːl 'lʌntʃɪz/
Science /'saɪəns/
Spanish /'spænɪʃ/
strict /strɪkt/
subject /'sʌbdʒɪkt/
terrible /'terəbl/
tomb /tuːm/

Unit 5

anglerfish /'æŋgləfɪʃ/
beach /biːtʃ/
boat /bəʊt/
bottom /'bɒtm/
cod /kɒd/
crab /kræb/
daylight /'deɪlaɪt/
deep /diːp/
dolphin /'dɒlfɪn/
fish /fɪʃ/
fish tank /'fɪʃ tæŋk/
freshwater /'freʃwɔːtə(r)/
frightened /'fraɪtnd/
jellyfish /'dʒelifɪʃ/
lake /leɪk/
lanternfish /'læntənfɪʃ/
leaflet /'liːflət/
octopus /'ɒktəpəs/
pike /paɪk/
ray /reɪ/
river /'rɪvə(r)/
saltwater /'sɒltwɔːtə(r)/
sand /sænd/
sardines /saːˈdiːnz/
sea /siː/
seahorse /'siːhɔːs/
shake /ʃeɪk/
shallow /'ʃæləʊ/
shark /ʃaːk/
shell /ʃel/
She was a star!
    /ʃiː wəz ə 'staː(r)/
show (n) /ʃəʊ/
starfish /'staːfɪʃ/
suncream /'sʌnkriːm/
surface /'sɜːfɪs/
trout /traʊt/
water (n) /'wɔːtə(r)/

Unit 6

bounce /baʊns/
burglar /'bɜːglə(r)/
camera /'kæmrə/
chase /tʃeɪs/
communicate /kə'mjuːnɪkeɪt/
computer /kəm'pjuːtə(r)/
drums /drʌmz/
explode /ɪk'spləʊd/
fireworks 'faɪəwɜːks/
flags /flægz/
giggle /'gɪgl/
horse /hɔːs/
Keep in touch. /kiːp ɪn 'tʌtʃ/
keyboard /'kiːbɔːd/
laptop /'læptɒp/
memory stick /'memri stɪk/
message /'mesɪdʒ/
mirrors /'mɪrəz/
mobile phone
   /məʊbaɪl 'fəʊn/
Morse code /mɔːs 'kəʊd/
mouse /maʊs/
newspaper /'njuːspeɪpə(r)/
pigeon /'pɪdʒɪn/
radio /'reɪdiəʊ/
screen /skriːn/
send /send/
smoke /sməʊk/
text message /'tekst mesɪdʒ/
thief, thieves /θiːf, θiːvz/
TV /tiː 'viː/
What happened?
   /wɒt 'hæpnd/
wriggle /'rɪgl/

Me and my world 2

competition /kɒmpə'tɪʃən/
diver /'daɪvə'r'/
diving /'daɪvɪŋ/
film director /'fɪlm daɪrektə'r'/
goggles /gɒglz/
inventor /ɪn'ventə'r'/
medal /'medəl/
Olympics /ə'lɪmpɪks/
underwater /ʌndə'wɔːtə'r'/

Unit 7

beans /biːnz/
bucket /'bʌkɪt/
cactus, cacti
   /'kæktəs, 'kæktaɪ/
cauliflower /'kɒlɪflaʊə(r)/
cold /kəʊld/
Don't forget to…
   /dəʊnt fə'get tə …/
dry /draɪ/
escape /ɪs'keɪp/
fern /fɜːn/
gate /geɪt/
goat /gəʊt/
Good work, kids!
   /gʊd 'wɜːk, kɪdz/
grass /graːs/
grow /grəʊ/
habitat /'hæbɪtæt/
hot /hɒt/
leaf, leaves /liːf, liːvz/
milk /mɪlk/
needle /'niːdl/
onions /'ʌnjənz/

Ouch, that hurts!
   /'aʊtʃ, ðæt 'hɜːts/
palm tree /'paːm triː/
peppers /'pepəz/
photosynthesis
   /fəʊtəʊ'sɪnθəsɪs /
pick /pɪk/
pine tree /'paɪn triː/
plant (v) /plaːnt/
potatoes /pə'teɪtəʊz/
seed /siːd/
shady /'ʃeɪdi/
spike /spaɪk/
strawberries /'strɔːbəriz/
sunflower /'sʌnflaʊə(r)/
sunny /'sʌni/
tap (n) /tæp/
tomatoes /tə'maːtəʊz/
water (v) /'wɔːtə(r)/
Watch out! /wɒtʃ 'aʊt/
weeds /wiːdz/
wet /wet/

Unit 8

bee /biː/
best /best/
beehive /'biːhaɪv/
big /bɪg/
collect /kə'lekt/
colony /'kɒləni/
comb /kəʊm/
camel /'kæməl/
drone /drəʊn/
elephant /'eləfənt/
fast /faːst/
frog /frɒg/
hippo /'hɪpəʊ/
honey /'hʌni/
kangaroo /kæŋgə'ruː/
lay eggs /leɪ 'egz/
mouse /maʊs/
nice /naɪs/
old /əʊld/
panda /'pændə/
polar bear /pəʊlə 'beə(r)/
queen /kwiːn/
short /ʃɔːt/
spider /'spaɪdə(r)/
swan /swɒn/
tortoise /'tɔːtəs/
worker /'wɜːkə(r)/
young /jʌŋ/

Me and my world 3

billion /'bɪljən/
bucket /'bʌkɪt/
bulb /bʌlb/
Canada /'kænədə/
fields /fiːldz/
Holland /'hɒlənd/
maple tree /'meɪpl triː/
maple syrup /meɪpl 'sɪrəp/
pancake /'pænkeɪk/
sap /sæp/
tulip /'tjuːlɪp/

Festival 1

World Car Free day /weːld caː(r)
'friː deɪ/
tandem /'tændəm/
trailer /'treɪlə(r)/
tram /træm/

Unit 9

120 one hundred and twenty
   /'wʌn hʌndrəd ən 'twenti/
360 three hundred and sixty
   /'θriː hʌndrəd ən 'sɪksti/
1,228 one thousand, two hundred
and twenty-eight
   /'wʌn θaʊznd tuː hʌndrəd ən
   twenti 'eɪt/
26,000 twenty-six thousand
   /'twenti sɪks 'θaʊznd/
Be careful! /bi 'keəfl/
bike /baɪk/
car /kaː(r)/
circus /'sɜːkəs/
city /'sɪti/
clown /klaʊn/
crazy /'kreɪzi/
Cross at the… /'krɒs ət ðə …/
crown /kraʊn/
cycling /'saɪklɪŋ/
distance /'dɪstəns/
gloves /glʌvz/
Go left at the…
   /gəʊ 'left ət ðə …/
Go right at the…
   /gəʊ 'raɪt ət ðə …/
helmet /'helmɪt/
Hold on tight.
   /həʊld ɒn 'taɪt/
How far…? /haʊ 'faː …/
How fast…? /haʊ 'faːst …/
How long…? /haʊ 'lɒŋ …/
(100) a hundred
   /ə 'hʌndrəd/
kilometres per hour
   /'kɪləmiːtə pə(r) 'aʊə(r)/
left /left/
Let's go! /lets 'gəʊ/
Look out! /lʊk 'aʊt/
right /raɪt/
road /rəʊd/
rule /ruːl/
Safety first! /'seɪfti 'fɜːst/
sign /saɪn/
speed /spiːd/
speed limit /spiːd 'lɪmɪt/
stop /stɒp/
Stop at the… /'stɒp ət ðə …/
(1000) a thousand
   /ə 'θaʊznd/
track /træk/
traffic lights /'træfɪk laɪts/
travel /'trævl/
Use your head! /juːz jə 'hed/
Watch out! /wɒtʃ 'aʊt/
zebra crossing
   /zebrə 'krɒsɪŋ/

OXFORD
UNIVERSITY PRESS

Great Clarendon Street, Oxford, OX2 6DP, United Kingdom

Oxford University Press is a department of the University of Oxford.
It furthers the University's objective of excellence in research, scholarship,
and education by publishing worldwide. Oxford is a registered trade
mark of Oxford University Press in the UK and in certain other countries

© Oxford University Press 2012

The moral rights of the author have been asserted

First published in 2012

2016

10 9 8

ISBN: 978 0 19 444231 2

Printed in China

This book is printed on paper from certified and well-managed sources

ACKNOWLEDGEMENTS

*The authors and publishers would like to thank the following teachers for their help in
developing the course:* Catherine Anner, Agnieszka Bajerlain, Sonia Bonjorn,
Rosario Brondolo, Claire Carril Rama and all at Colegio Alca in Milladoiro,
Beata Chmielewska, Joanna Cudowska-Kolendo, Karolina Gogolewska, Joanna
Herok, Aine Kiely, Gladys Ledwith, Silvia Luppi, Magdalena Łapczuk, Julie
Mills, Izabela Pastewska, Szymon Polakowski, Ewa Rowińska, Richard Savage.

Main illustrations by: Paul Gibbs pp.2, 3, 6, 7, 11, 14, 19, 22, 23, 29, 32, 37, 40, 45,
48, 55, 58, 63, 66, 71, 74, 81, 82, 83

Pronunciation chant illustrations by: Dave Whammond/3 in a Box pp.10, 18, 26,
36, 44, 52, 62, 70, 78

Story illustrations by: Paul Gibbs and John Haslam pp.4, 5, 12, 13, 20, 21, 30, 31,
38, 39, 46, 47, 56, 57, 64, 65, 72, 73

Cambridge Young Learners illustrations by: Judy Brown pp.84, 85, 86, 87, 88, 89,
90, 91

Other illustrations by: Kathy Baxendale p.17; Adrian Barclay/Beehive Illustration
pp.8, 9, 24, 56, 60, 61, 69; James Elston pp.15, 33, 49, 59, 67; John Haslam
pp.28, 54, 80; Brian Lee pp.27, 53, 75, 79; Myles Talbot pp.42, 43

Cover illustration by: Paul Gibbs

Commissioned photography by: Gareth Boden pp.10, 18, 24, 25, 26, 36, 44, 52, 62,
70, 78

*The Publishers would also like to thank the following for their kind permission to
reproduce photographs and other copyright material:* Alamy pp.61 (Cosmo Condina/
sunflowers), 15 (CandyBox Photography/cyclist), 33 (Thislife Pictures/school,
1940s), (ClassicStock/school, 1960s), (Peter Titmuss/school, modern), 34 (Rolf
Richardson/Great Pyramid), (bygonetimes/Egyptian pharaoh), 35 (bygonetimes/
Egyptian god Horus), (Gary Cook/Egyptian god Sobek), (The Art Gallery
Collection/Egyptian goddess Bastet), 41 (Bill Bachman/marine life at Water
World), (Brandon Cole Marine Photography/dolphins), (Brandon Cole Marine
Photography/jellyfish), (Stephen Frink Collection/sharks), 42 (David R. Frazier
Photolibrary, Inc/fish), 59 (Art Directors & TRIP/farm in Spain), (Big Cheese
Photo LLC/family on farm), 61 (CuboImages srl/cactus), (Chad Ehlers/ferns),
76 (WoodyStock/speedometer), 77 (Motoring Picture Library/domestic car),
(SUNNYphotography.com/plane), 79 (Megapress/boy); Ardea p.68 (Steve Hopkin/
queen bee); Bigstockphoto p.27 (keeweeboy/African boy); Corbis pp.27 (Ocean/
meerkats), 34 (Sandro Vannini/Egyptian god Khnum), (Free Agents Limited/
Egyptian goddess Nephthys), 35 (Gianni Dagli Orti/Egyptian god Osiris), (Roger
Wood/Egyptian god Isis), (Sandro Vannini/Egyptian goddess Tefnut), 50 (Hulton-
Deutsch Collection/mirrors), (Bettmann/semaphore), (Bettmann/pony express),
(Bettmann/pigeon); FLPA p.68 (Michael Durham/Minden Pictures/worker bee);
Fotolia p.79 (Mat Hayward/girl with tulip bulbs); Getty Images pp.16 (Gregor
Schuster/Photonica/Big Ben), (Stephen Alvarez/National Geographic/Eiffel
tower), 17 (Stephen Alvarez/National Geographic/Eiffel tower), 50 (Meyer
Pfundt/Hulton Archive/telegraph operator), 68 (Anita Oberhauser/Stockfood
Creative/honey and comb), 76 (Jamal Nasrallah/Thrust car), 77 (Jim Cummins/
Taxi/person walking), (Andy Rouse/Stone/cheetah), (Vladimir Rys/Bongarts/
racing car), (Frank Whitney/The Image Bank/space shuttle); iStockphoto
pp.27 (Jbryson/girl), 49 (RimDream/Alex rollerblading), (suemack/Alex on
waterslide), 61 (RonTech2000/palm tree); The Kobal Collection p.53 (Turner
Network Television/Jacque Cousteau underwater with camera); Lonely Planet
Images p.16 (Jonathan Smith/Palace of Science, Warsaw); Mary Evans Picture
Library p.50 (smoke signals), (drums); Nature Picture Library p.42 (David Shale/
angler fish); Oxford University Press p.67 (Corbis/Digital Stock/hippo), (Digital
Vision/lion); Photolibrary pp.15 (Pixtal Images/man at computer), 79 (Radius
Images/tulips); Rex Features p.53 (Agencia Keystone/Jacques Cousteau on
boat), (Olycom SPA/Tom Daley with medal), (South West News Service/Tom
Daley diving); Shutterstock pp.16 (Fedor Selivanov/leaning tower of Pisa),
34 (Mikhail Zahranichny/Egyptian mummy), 42 (cbpix/clownfish in anemone),
49 (muzsy/Alex playing football), 53 (Zurijeta/boy), (Monkey Business Images/
girl), 61 (cla78/pine trees), 67 (Hung Chung Chih/panda), 68 (costall/beehive),
(alle/drone bee), 79 (GoodMood Photo/bucket on maple trunk), (Brandon
Blinkenberg/bottle of maple syrup); Thomas Mayer Archive p.16 (Sapphire of
Istanbul); VolcanoDiscovery p.27 (Tom Pfeiffer/Hekla volcano)

THE MEON VALLEY RAILWAY

Revisited

Denis Tillman

KRB Publications

KRB Publications
2 Denewulf Close
BISHOPS WALTHAM
Hants
SO32 1GZ

ISBN 0954203542

Printed by the Amadeus Press

Front Cover:- At Wickham in 1952 an up Push-Pull, Set No. 3 passes a down goods hauled by T9 No. 30310. (Denis Callender)

Contents

Preface

Did you ever! Me writing a book! There's a first time for everything I suppose and after much prodding from Kevin I am about to embark on a project, which, I hope, will provide, both myself, and my readers, with some new information and a photographic record of the route.

The project began as a result of an offer to my local museum to mount a display in 2003 to celebrate the centenary of the line in a similar manner to two previous exhibitions. The first celebrated 150 years of the coming of the railway to Fareham and the other the 150th anniversary of the opening of the Fareham to Portsmouth route. Much information had been accumulated, and more was becoming available, so the suggestion was that some of the previously unpublished photographs could be put together to form the basis of a small publication. Kevin had recently started his own publishing business, so the pressure was on to come up with some text to accompany the photographs, a few maps and a diagram or two, and, hopefully, you will find the result both informative and interesting.

Since the publication of Ray Stone's book in 1983, many new photographs and information has come to light and it is this previously unpublished material that forms the backbone of this book.

Acknowledgements

Thanks for information and photographs are due to Denis Callender, Denis Cullum, Hugh Davies, Ron French, Kevin Robertson, Malcolm Snellgrove, Peter Swift, G.A. Tull, M. Walshaw, The Hampshire Record Office and Wickham Community Centre. I am especially grateful to The South Western Circle which has an archive service available to members including a Portfolio on the Meon Valley Railway. Finally thanks must go to my long suffering wife who kept me typing and my daughters who rescued the text after the computer crashed and taught me a few more computer skills along the way.

The Meon Valley Railway

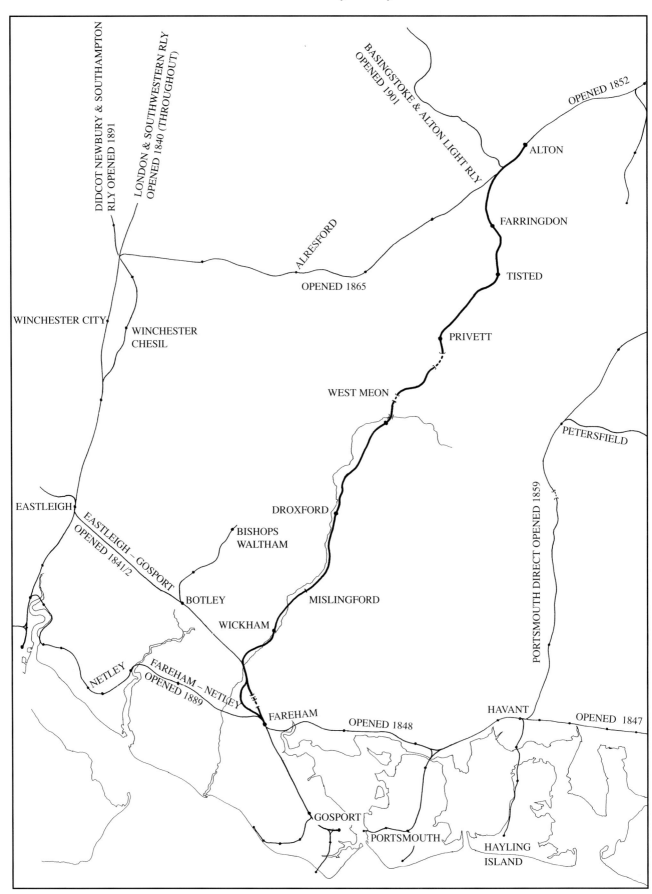

DIDCOT NEWBURY & SOUTHAMPTON RLY OPENED 1891

LONDON & SOUTHWESTERN RLY OPENED 1840 (THROUGHOUT)

BASINGSTOKE & ALTON LIGHT RLY OPENED 1901

OPENED 1852

ALTON

FARRINGDON

TISTED

ALRESFORD

OPENED 1865

PRIVETT

WINCHESTER CITY

WINCHESTER CHESIL

WEST MEON

PETERSFIELD

PORTSMOUTH DIRECT OPENED 1859

EASTLEIGH

EASTLEIGH – GOSPORT OPENED 1841/2

DROXFORD

BISHOPS WALTHAM

MISLINGFORD

BOTLEY

WICKHAM

NETLEY

FAREHAM – NETLEY OPENED 1889

FAREHAM

OPENED 1848

HAVANT

OPENED 1847

GOSPORT

PORTSMOUTH

HAYLING ISLAND

The Meon Valley Railway

During the 1800s there were several schemes to construct a railway through the Meon Valley area (see map opposite). These started as far back as 1845, with a proposal to build a line from Southampton, through Petersfield and onto London. Six years later a scheme to construct a line from Alton to Petersfield was considered, followed three years later by the Alton Extension Railway.

In 1859/60 there were at least six different proposals for a route from Petersfield to Botley, via Bishops Waltham, followed by a Havant, Hambledon and Droxford Railway of 1864/5, a Windsor, Aldershot and Portsmouth Railway in 1881, a Basingstoke, Alton and Petersfield line in 1883, a Basingstoke, East Hants and Portsmouth railway in 1887 and finally a Bishops Waltham Light Railway to Brockbridge in 1899.

One objector to the Havant, Hambledon and Droxford Railway is recorded as stating that the line would 'anihilate (sic) the hunting'.

But in 1897 a proposal was laid before Parliament by the London and South Western Railway that showed a line running from Alton to Fareham. Deviating from the Alton to Winchester line at Butts junction, the route was to run via Farringdon (originally spelt Faringdon), Tisted, Privett, West Meon, Droxford and Wickham to a new junction on the Eastleigh and Bishopstoke[1] to Fareham line to be known as Knowle Junction. Estimated at a total cost of £348,214 5s 2d, the contractor, Messrs. Relfe & Son of Plymouth, commenced work in 1898 on the chalk cuttings, the spoil from which was used in the construction of the embankments.

In order to avoid Fareham Tunnel, as the soil through which the tunnel had been built proved to be unstable, a new line was also to be constructed from Knowle Junction, deviating to the west from the original route to Fareham rejoining the line immediately north of the Netley and Southampton route out of Fareham at an estimated cost of £35,329 9s 2d. Once this deviation line had been constructed and maintenance work on the tunnel undertaken, the Meon Valley Line trains used the then singled line through the tunnel to gain access to Fareham. Even this deviation line proved unstable and was finally closed in 1973 prior to the construction of the south coast motorway (M27). This work necessitated the lengthening of the northern end of Fareham Tunnel where the contractor experienced similar problems with the soil conditions.

The final piece of engineering works to complete the line was for the widening of the route from Alton to Butts junction at an estimated cost of £15,956 7s 11d, making a grand total of just under £400,000. The route opened on 1st June 1903.

I make no excuse for the fact that, although all previous works on the subject have described the line as the Alton to Fareham line, I will be describing it, as per the official London and South Western Railway Terrier description for the line, as the 'Fareham to Alton' line, and will deal with the route geographically in that order. Anyway, I live at the south end and have always considered it to be that way round!

So let's get started....

[1] Formerly known as Bishopstoke from the opening of the Southampton to Winchester line on 10 June 1839 until the end of 1852, when it became Bishopstoke Junction, to be renamed again in July 1889 as Eastleigh and Bishopstoke and finally to be renamed Eastleigh in July 1923.
(The History of the Southern Railway by C F Dendy Marshall)

To administer to the spiritual and social welfare needs of the navvies, a travelling mission from The Church Army accompanied the men as they slowly traversed the route. Camps were set up at various locations including one where the original name persists today in the form of the 'West Meon Hut'. A group of navvies is seen here near to Droxford and taking a break during the construction with the 'Preacher' much in evidence in the centre of the front row.

Hampshire Record Office.
217M84/7

Fareham, on the last day of passenger working, 5th February 1955, sees a four-coach train waiting in the bay, platform 1, having just arrived from Alton. The M7, No 30055, will shortly run round its train ready for the return journey. An interesting point to note is that at least the two coaches nearest the camera are in lined carmine livery. If there had been as many passengers as this on a normal operating day the line may well still be open today! (Denis Callender)

FAREHAM

The M7, having run-round its train takes water before the return working to Alton.

(G. A. Tull, South Western Circle)

Above: Push-pull set No 4, on an Alton to Fareham service approaching the bay platform at Fareham in 1949. (Denis Callender)

Right: Looking through the north portal of Fareham Tunnel clearly shows the two sections of the tunnel. The gap in the middle was caused by the collapse of the tunnel prior to the opening of the Eastleigh to Gosport line. Just four days after it opened on 29th November 1841 further slippage of the clay through which the tunnel had been dug caused the line to be closed, to be re-opened on 7th February 1842. (Denis Callender)

Seven acres of land had been acquired from Knowle Asylum, at a cost of £846 12s. 0d (£846.60) for the land and £130 for the loss of crops, by the London & South Western Railway in 1897 in preparation for the building of the Meon Valley Railway. Sidings had previously been provided when the Asylum, which had been opened in 1852, built a gas plant in 1881. In 1901 a coal fired electric generating plant was installed and although converted to oil firing in 1958 the siding was still used for off loading coal in the 1960's. One amusing incident recorded in 1935 is that of an inmate of Knowle Hospital who was found walking the line at Droxford apparently on his way to London to see the Prince of Wales to tell him about all the foreigners in Knowle.

KNOWLE HALT AND SIDING

Left: Knowle Halt in 1952. Opened on 1st May 1907 as Knowle Asylum Halt and closed in 1964 by which time it was known as just plain Knowle. With a platform length only suitable for two-coach trains, for many years it was only served by Meon Valley line trains but after 1955 the occasional main line train called. (Denis Callender)

Lower: A busy scene at 'Knowle' shortly before closure, clearly showing the barley twist lamp columns with electric lighting fitted. Knowle was one of the first stations in the area to have electric lighting, power being supplied by the hospital generators. (Lens)

KNOWLE JUNCTION

An unidentified T9 leaves the Meon Valley line approaching Knowle, the tall signal at the end of the branch clearly visible. The brick arched viaduct, spanning the River Meon, over which it is crossing, was widened during the construction of the deviation line avoiding Fareham Tunnel to accommodate the extra track having been originally built for the double track Eastleigh to Gosport line in 1841. (Denis Callender)

Before we start our journey up the Meon Valley line proper let's take a peek inside Knowle junction signal box where we find the signalman working a Stevens' frame with 25 levers (although by this time 10 were spare). Knowle box opened with the line in 1903 and closed just short of its 70th anniversary having seen no less than 7 changes of track layout, three of which occurred in its first 4 years with another three in its last 9 years of use. It finally closed in May 1973 with the singling of the Botley to Fareham line. (South Western Circle)

Inset: Having taken the tablet for the Knowle Junction to Wickham section we are off up the Valley on the last day of passenger operation. (G. A. Tull, South Western Circle)

Here we see the 8.50am Eastleigh to Portsmouth and Southsea van train passing Knowle Junction on 13 March 1961. Immediately behind N15 class locomotive No 30804 'Sir Cador of Cornwall' the leading vehicle is interesting in the fact that it is one of the ex ferry train vehicles which were transferred to general stock when withdrawn from ferry service. A small platform can be seen to the rear of the box where the Tyler's No 6 Tablet to Wickham would have been exchanged. (L Elsey.)

On the southern approaches to Wickham Station the line crosses two road bridges and two river bridges. The first of the road bridges spanned Fareham Road, where we see an early idyllic rural scene with several of the locals posing for the photographer. To make way for the railway, several cottages had to be demolished on the south side of this road. (Wickham Community Centre)

Having crossed the River Meon once and then the two road accesses into Wickham village from the east, the line then crossed back over the river immediately south of the station. Here we see the navvies - I was going to say hard at work but they have all stopped work to pose for the photographer during the construction of the bridge. (G. A. Tull, South Western Circle)

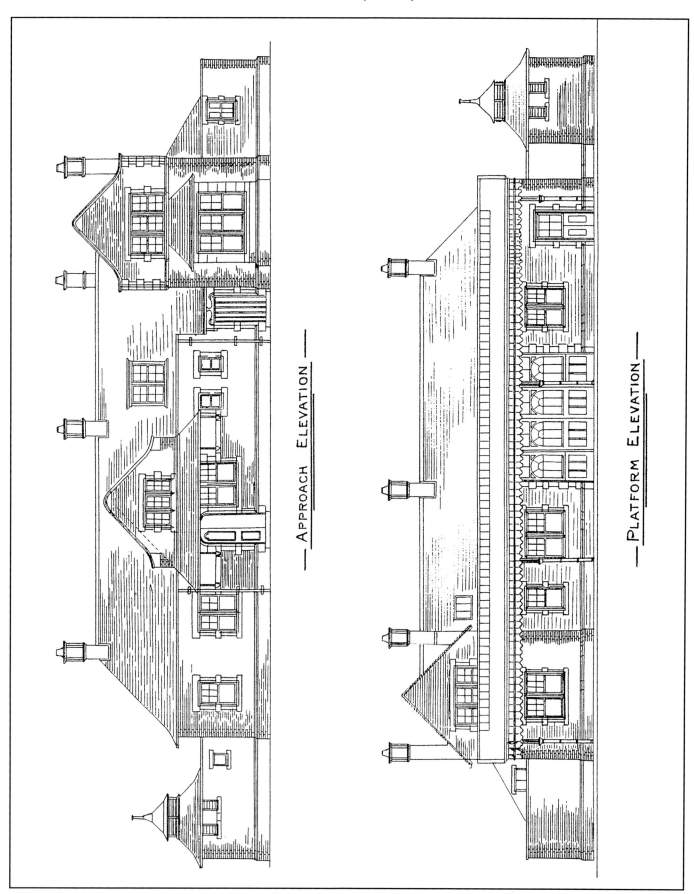

APPROACH ELEVATION

PLATFORM ELEVATION

Wickham Station as built, with standard London & South Western diagonal fencing and a pristine white painted gate into the goods yard area. All the stations were to a standard design but were handed. The handing was not dependent on whether the station buildings were on the up side or the down side of the line nor whether they were at the Alton end or the Fareham end of the building but were dependent on the booking office being at the nearest end to the approach road making the station masters accommodation furthest from the approach road. (British Rail / Kidderminster Railway Museum)

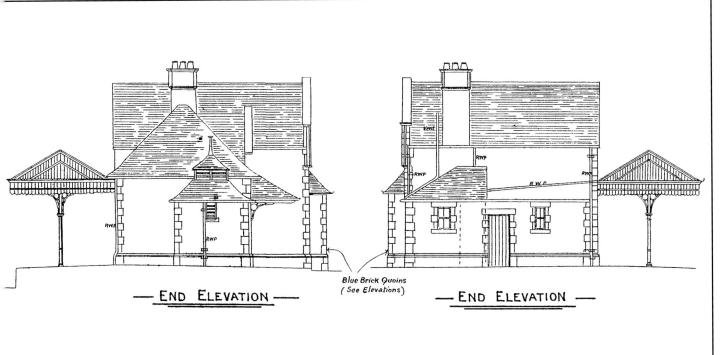

— END ELEVATION —

Blue Brick Quoins
(See Elevations)

— END ELEVATION —

Above: In 1952, having waited for the up Push-Pull set to pass (see front cover), T9 No 30310 is free to continue its journey south towards Fareham immediately crossing the River Meon where we see that the bridge was constructed to take double track. The ex private owner wagon behind the tender is interesting in that it still retains the original livery of 'Bolsover' colliery but it was taken into stock in 1948, as all privately owned wagons were, and given a P prefixed number, in this case P321213. Many such wagons lasted into the 1960's still retaining their, by then, very faded original liveries. (Denis Callender)

Left: Viewed through the station north towards Alton in 1930. At this stage the footbridge still remained although it would be removed shortly afterwards as a maintenance economy measure a few years later leaving passengers to use the board crossing at the Alton end of the platforms.

(G.A. Tull, South Western Circle.)

Above left: Although a bit blurred this picture, taken in the 1930's, has been included because it shows an Adams Jubilee Class locomotive on a down passenger train at Wickham. It is known that this class of locomotive was regularly used on the Meon Valley route especially in the early days when through trains from Waterloo to Gosport used the line. Signalman Willsher is walking down the platform ready to hand over the Wickham to Knowle Junction tablet. (G A Tull, South Western Circle)

Above right: A 1952 view, this time showing the signal box, telegraph pole and lamp. The original wooden palisade fence has been replaced with standard Southern Railway concrete post and wire whilst the signal box nameboard is also in standard green and cream albeit somewhat faded. (Denis Callender)

Another early view of Wickham showing the standard wooden footbridge and signal box designs used throughout the line. (Lens)

A view from the up platform, at the south end of the station building, showing the down platform passenger shelter. The large opening onto the platform was bricked in during the second world war with only a standard door opening remaining presumably for use as a basic bomb shelter. Wickham village was very much a self contained community until the advent of the private motor car made it possible to work further afield. Accordingly up to about 1930 at least three coal merchants were reported as receiving supplies at the station. These were H.T. Clements 'Carrier & Coal Merchant', Edney Bros, 'Coal & Corn Merchant' who traded from the High Street, and also from 1927 to 1931 Wm. Fred. Churcher 'Coal Merchant. Also mentioned as dealing in fuel within the Wickham area was Mrs. Flora Bailey, although it is not known if supplies for this person were received at the station. The station and yard would also deal with much in the way of other locally required and produced goods including those from Wickham Mill. There was also a brewery at Wickham and for some years an Iron and Brass foundry - run in 1907 by Wm. Wheatley. Soft fruit in season, particularly strawberries were handled in quantity at both Wickham and at Mislingford.
(Kevin Robertson Collection)

Looking south from the north end of the down platform we can clearly see that the footbridge has been removed. Passengers were now required to use the barrow crossing at the north end of the platforms in order to cross the line under the watchful eye of the signalman. (Denis Callender)

On 27th January 1955 the concrete running in board reminds us we are still at Wickham, this time looking north from the up platform. The barrow crossing used by passengers can be seen, and beyond the end of the platform can be seen a small shed. (Denis Cullum)

Left: By the time of BR Wickham permanent way gang had use of this pre-war built Wickham trolley, No DS 3008, which was used by the platelayers to travel up and down their section of line. These sheds appear at all the other stations on the line, but did they all contain a motorised trolley?
(Denis Callender)

Below: Over the years several storage sheds were built in the goods yard to supplement the original facilities which consisted of just the corrugated building with awning. The extra buildings also give a good indication as to the volume of traffic handled at the line's peak. Most of the new buildings were built off the ground so, if used for grain, prevented damp and afforded some protection against vermin.
(South Western Circle)

Above: Travelling north from Wickham the line passes under the A32 main Fareham to Alton road…………..
(Denis Callender)

.....before arriving at Mislingford where a Maunsell Mogul bursts forth from under the next bridge up the line on its way to Droxford. It was here, during WW2, that a temporary wooden platform was constructed to serve the Canadian Army, which was camped in the Forest of Bere. The goods yard here was used in the build up to D-Day with the delivery of tanks and other vehicles which were then stored, on concrete laybys, some of which still exist today, in the lanes around the area, before being loaded, at places like Stokes Bay, onto landing craft ready for the invasion. A pallet van can be seen in one of the sidings. (Ron French)

MISLINGFORD

Two railwayman's cottages were provided at Mislingford. Built to a standard design for the line they provided what, in their day, was modern and comfortable accommodation. The wind pump in the back garden pumped water up from a well to the water tank to provide a gravity fed water supply. (Ron French)

The rear view of the cottages, taken from the top of the wind pump, shows the lean-to building which housed the copper boiler and the bucket toilet. (Ron French)

After the closure of the line to passenger traffic in 1955, the centre section of the line, from Droxford to Farringdon, was lifted. The southern section was retained until 30th April 1962 for goods traffic and here we see a sugar beet train hauled by a Class C2X heading south passing Mislingford sidings. (Ron French)

Looking south on New Years Day 1955 from the access into Mislingford sidings we can see that the sidings could only be shunted by up trains. At this time the ground frame to the left controlled only the points, the shunting signals having been removed on 27th May 1945. The goods yard at Mislingford was originally provided with a goods shed, but it was destroyed by fire when the adjoining timber yard caught fire in 1938. The fire burned for a week. (Denis Cullum)

On 30th April 1961 the Solent Limited, double headed by Class E1 No 32694 and Class O2 No 30200, passes the cottages. (Ron French)

After closure in 1962 Mr Charles Ashby, based at Droxford, used the line as a test bed for his 'Pacerailer' railbus. In 1963 he acquired A1X Class Terrier No 32646, which can be seen here on one of its trips to Wickham and back. Having run low on water a garden hose from one of the cottages provides a welcome drink while young Master French looks on. The Terrier was sold to Brickwoods in 1966 to be mounted on a plinth outside their public house 'Hayling Billy' on Hayling Island. Thankfully this locomotive has now been returned to working order and can be seen on the Isle of Wight Steam Railway based at Havenstreet. (Ron French)

In 1965 the Southern Locomotive Preservation Company came to an agreement with Mr Ashby to store some of their stock at Droxford and in 1969 rescued USA Class tank No 30064 can be seen here hauling their GWR Toad brake van and Maunsell coach. (Ron French)

Shortly after opening an up train waits to head north. The shadows falling on the opposite platform indicate that the coaches are formed into a 4½ set (four bogie coaches and one six-wheel passenger brake van) with the set number, 36, displayed on the end. Unfortunately no records survive to verify this. This coaching formation was common on the line in its early days, the first train, hauled by an Adams Radial tank, being formed of such a set. As early as 1907 the 'Colliery Supply Co.' is recorded as having coal staithes at the station, although any monopoly this organisation had was to be short lived for by 1911 the firm of 'I.W. Knight' was also reported as dealing with solid fuel. Another organisation, 'Read & Sons' is reported in 1923 and around the same time, and until at least 1939, 'J.E. Smith (Portsmouth) Ltd.' was at the station. The last named was also known to run its own wagons. The actual coal office was located on the back approach road to the yard and had, it was said, 300-400 tons of coal stacked in the yard at any one time. Additionally, general agricultural produce was handled. Also in the period prior to 1914, most of the goods supplied to the local shops, would arrive by rail. This would of course have applied also at the other villages along the route. At Droxford cattle were dealt with whilst beer from the Courage Brewery at Alton was delivered for the Station Hotel on the east side of the station. In later years sugar beet was also an important commodity. (Hampshire Record Office)

DROXFORD

Above: Arriving at Droxford we find the carpenters proudly standing on their newly completed footbridge.

Lower: The 2.48pm Fareham to Alton train enters the south end of the station on 4th December 1954. Above the station nameboard can be seen the remaining pair of railway cottages. There were originally four cottages here but during WW2 a bomb severely damaged two which were subsequently demolished. (Both - South Western Circle)

Troop movements on the line started very early in its history and here we find the 5th Isle of Wight 'Princess Beatrice's' Volunteer Brigade Hants Regt. forming up outside Droxford station on 21st May 1904 ready to march off to their training camp. The railway company constructed the road, on which they are standing, as a diversion to the original route that was buried under the railway. (Hampshire Record Office 217M84/56/26)

Centre: On 8th December 1914 the British Navy, under Admiral Sturdee, was victorious over the German admiral von Spee at the Battle of the Falklands. Here we see Admiral Sturdee returning to Droxford with Lady Sturdee preceding him over the footbridge. (Hampshire Record Office 217M84/56/55)

Left: On arrival on the platform, he was greeted by Mrs Nellie Reeves, the local press agent and Droxford shopkeeper. (Hampshire Record Office217M84/50/25)

"A busy scene at Droxforf with an up goods hauled by '700' class No. 30305 crossing the down push-pull service on a cold winters day. (S.L.S.Collection.)"

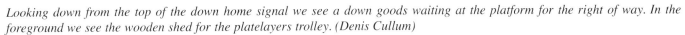

Looking down from the top of the down home signal we see a down goods waiting at the platform for the right of way. In the foreground we see the wooden shed for the platelayers trolley. (Denis Cullum)

Another wintry scene and which highlights the slightly unusual shape of the roof line. The lack of footprints and snow clearance from the platform edge (See previous page) indicates an early morning view. (S.L.S. Collection.)

On 26th March 1962 Class T9, after repair at Eastleigh works, re-entered revenue earning service in South Western Urie livery. Two days later we see her shunting at Droxford in the hands of driver Les Hiscock. This locomotive is now preserved. (Ron French)

In Droxford goods yard the, presumably original, 5-ton crane still stands in the early 1970's. The plate indicates that it was provided by 'T Lanmuth & Co. Engineers Manchester'. The lorries in the background are labelled 'Road Transport Industry Training Board'. (South Western Circle)

An unusual bridge, near Corhampton, which, although of standard design, provides passage for river, road and pedestrians. 1949 (Denis Callender)

The 1.30pm Alton to Fareham train near Meonstoke on the 4th December 1954. (South Western Circle)

WESTMEON. 139.

An early view of West Meon Station taken from the tower of the parish church shows the station building with, to the left, the goods shed and various goods vehicles in the sidings and, to the right the signal box. The postcard from which this picture was taken was posted in 1907 but the clean white chalk surfaces to the cuttings indicate a date very shortly after opening. Together with the stations at Droxford and Wickham, West Meon was of similar importance in so far as the amount of traffic handled whilst in addition acting as a railhead for the similarly named East Meon village some 3 miles distant. As with Droxford, the 'Colliery Supply Company' was reported to have been trading from the location as early as 1907 whilst in addition 'I. W. Knight' was listed in 1911. After this time the only name relative to coal was Messrs Stone. Other goods traffic included for some time locally grown potatoes destined for pig feed, which would be sprayed with a blue dye to indicate they were unfit for human consumption. Milk was also handled from several local farms and regularly sent to the Portsea Island Co-op. An unusual traffic was empty wooden coffins regularly received covered in sack cloth from an unknown maker. These were initially destined to an East Meon Undertaker. Cattle was another very important traffic and vans to deal with this were often seen in the yard. Such vehicles would be sent in both north and south directions. (Author's Collection)

WEST MEON

This page, top: The station during construction, the concrete platforms being laid with no sign yet of the wooden footbridge.
Lower: Complete and open for business!
(Both South Western Circle)

Probably not long after the opening of the line, a group of passengers awaits a Fareham service on the down platform. The young boy in the foreground clearly could not remain still during the necessarily long film exposure of the period! The conical milk churns on the platform confirm this type of traffic whilst both the barrow and lamp glass display the station name. (South Western Circle)

Two views from the same aspect, the upper early view shows the starter signal and water column at the end of the platform, a platelayers hut by the cattle pens, palisade fencing to the platforms and the row of six railway cottages. (South Western Circle)

A similar view taken in the 1950's, which at first glance shows little seems to have changed. The starting signal was re-sited 40 yards nearer the signal box on 19th October 1922. Was this the time that the footbridge was removed and the usable platform length reduced and what happened to the water column? It would mean that trains would be stopped prior to the dip in the platform and that passengers could now cross the line within sight of the signalman. (Incidentally all the distant signals on this route were changed by the Southern Railway from red to yellow arms in 1928.) The platform fencing is now concrete post and wire and a wooden shed for the platelayers' trolley has appeared.
(N. Simmonds/H. Davis)

Left: Another, earlier, view from the road, showing the trackside of the buildings. It also shows the deep cutting, which appears so white in the view from the church tower. (South Western Circle)

Right: On 9th June 1954 700 Class No 30308 is seen approaching with the 6.48pm Fareham to Alton goods. The tunnel under the platform which carried the point rodding and signal wires from the signal box can be seen. (Denis Cullum)

Left: A New Years Day 1955 view of the southern approaches from the top of the up home signal shows the track layout, which was similar for all the stations on the line. (Denis Cullum)

Left: The station buildings seen from the road on 1st January 1955 showing the approach road side. (Denis Cullum)

Right: Again approaching from the south, a very short goods train hauled by 700 Class No 30350. This photograph shows the steps provided to gain access to the shortened platform section. (South Western Circle)

Left: We catch up again with the last train down from Alton as it simmers at the platform before heading south. (R Barnard)

Right top: On 23rd January 1955 the 'West Meon Meteor', having off loaded its ramblers, now heads south, with name board removed, behind Class D1 No 31739. (South Western Circle) (A photograph of this same train can be found on page 60 of 'The Railways of Gosport' by Kevin Robertson.)

On the last day of operation M7 No 30055 takes water from the only water column on the route. (G A Tull, South Western Circle)

Lower: On Sunday 6th February 1955, the day following the official closure there was a final moment of glory with the RCTS special, 'The Hampshireman', behind two Class T9s 30301 and 30732 seen heading north. (Hampshire Chronicle)

WEST MEON VIADUCT
AND THE TUNNELS

Above: Just round the corner we find T9 No 30705 approaching with the 10.20am goods from Alton to Fareham on 4th December 1954. The top of the viaduct can be seen in the background.
(South Western Circle)

Left: A view from track level on 19th June 1954 shows that the viaduct was built for double track.
(Denis Cullum)

Viaduct West Meon

The original design for the viaduct was for an eight arch concrete structure, work on which was actually started until it was found that the soil at the south end would not bear the weight. The decision was then made to reduce the length of the structure to just four arches but this time with steel piers and arches supported on massive concrete bases. Each span of the revised design was to the same length as that originally proposed and so in effect reduced the overall length of the viaduct by half. Accordingly, at the southern approach the embankment was extended, presumably over the four now redundant bases. One may wonder if it had been constructed solely in concrete, whether it would still be standing today like the Cannington Viaduct on the Axminster to Lyme Regis Branch. Incidentally the Cannington Viaduct built at about the same time as West Meon, suffered subsidence during construction, which may also have influenced the decision to change the method of construction of our subject. (Author's collection)

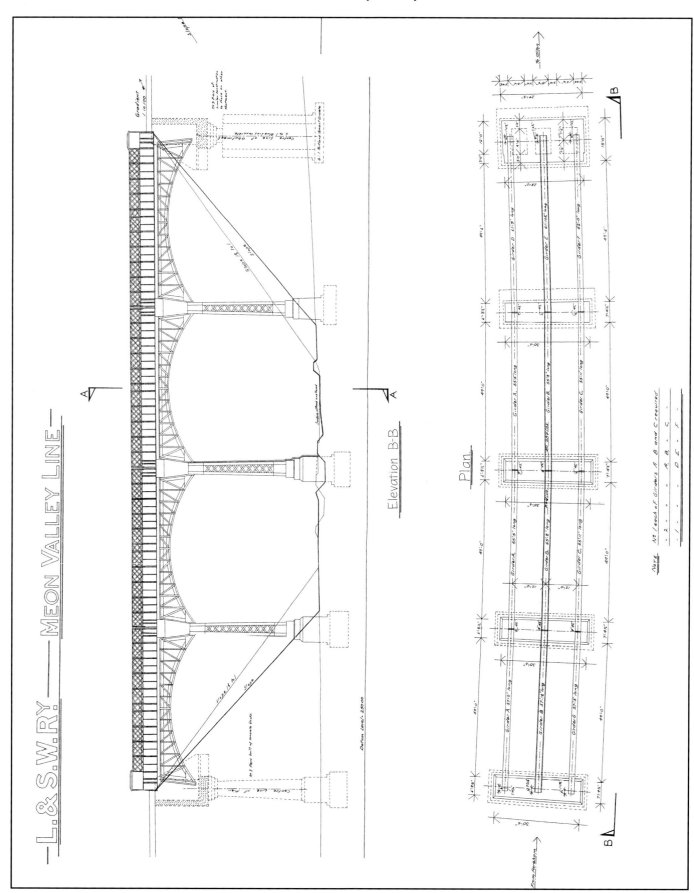

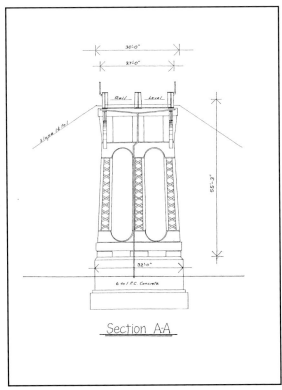

Section A-A

A view taken, in 1951, from the train north of the viaduct clearly shows that it was built on a curve. In the background can be seen the six railway cottages built to the east of the railway and the large water tank which fed the cottages, the station and the water columns. (Denis Callender)

Two views along the viaduct, one prior to demolition 19th June 1954 and….(Denis Cullum)

…… one during demolition. (M H Walshaw / H. Davis)

Opposite page, top: Looking back from the top of the viaduct we can see the church tower and the rest of the village laid out before us, a view that had not been seen prior to the coming of the railway. (Author's collection)

Opposite page, lower: Taken from West Meon Church tower, this time showing, in the distance, the viaduct, with, what looks like, an M7 with a three-coach train. (Author's collection)

Once over the viaduct we shortly enter West Meon Tunnel, (above)539 yards long, ...

.....out the other end (left) and ....

.... over the Petersfield Road (right) where the road tunnel is 167 feet long. To the north of this road was one of the navvy encampments. (all three South Western Circle)

Right: Thence into Privett Tunnel, 1056 yards in length. Although the tunnels were constructed to take double track the cuttings were not. (Denis Callender)

Lower: "Passing the arm less signal post which was originally the up distant for Privett, the arm having been removed some 30 years previous....."
(S.L.S.)

PRIVETT

……to arrive at Privett, the highest point on the line at 519 feet above sea level. (South Western Circle)

A view of the southern approaches from bridge No 25 reveals in the distance the six railway cottages built on the opposite side of the Gosport Road to the station. (Denis Cullum)

A view up the approach road shows the standard station building. There must be some considerable doubt as to the viability of a stopping place here at all as the village after which it was named was some little distance away and in reality was little more than a hamlet. Originally the stopping place was to have been 'West Tisted' - indeed it is located within that parish, but that name was not chosen to avoid confusion with Tisted Station. Traffic handled was always limited even by Meon Valley standards, with no coal merchant listed although some staithes and a small office are shown on a 1909 plan. (South Western Circle)

Taken shortly after opening this view is taken from the new access road, built by the railway company, which gave a direct link to Basing Park Farm. A new public house, then known as 'The Privett Bush', visible in the background, was built on the Gosport Road in the hope that the railway would bring some welcome customers. (South Western Circle)

Early maintenance of the wooden footbridge would give modern Health and Safety Inspectors something to worry about. No extending ladders in those days so you put two together and tie them securely with ropes! An item of note is the white sighting board for the up starter. (South Western Circle)

Right: The signal box at Privett still looks well kept in 1951 even though it has only acted as a ground frame since the tablet section was abolished on 20th June 1922 and the up platform and loop taken out of use. (Denis Callender)

Lower: A down train, consisting of push-pull set No 4, coasts into the station on its way from Alton. (South Western Circle)

Left: The 'West Meon Meteor' stops at Privett on 23rd January 1955 where some of the ramblers on board disembark (R Barnard / H. Davis)

Opposite right: M7 No 54 leaves Privett with an up push-pull service in 1949. (South Western Circle)

Opposite lower: 700 Class No 30692 heads the 12.23pm Alton to Fareham on 18th December 1954. (South Western Circle)

'The Hampshireman' tops the summit of the line on the day after official closure. Having left Waterloo at 9.45am behind H2 Class Atlantic No 32421 the train travelled via Hounslow, Chertsey and Woking to Guildford, where the Atlantic was replaced by two E5X Class engines, 32570 and 32576. From Guildford the train travelled to Petersfield via Cranleigh, Horsham, Pulborough and Midhurst. At Petersfield another exchange of engines saw the two T9's, 30301 and 30732, in charge for the final leg via Havant, Fareham, West Meon, Alton Aldershot, Frimley, Farnborough and eventually back to Waterloo. In the words of Wallace and Grommit 'A grand day out'. (South Western Circle)

The southern approach to Tisted was on a curve and in a deep cutting so a tall home signal was provided so train crews had the best possible forward sighting. (Denis Callender)

M7 No 30054 and push-pull set No 4 on a down train leave Tisted heading for Privett. (South Western Circle)

The front of Tisted station with its 'Fareham' chimney pots. Tisted, or be to more precise East Tisted, served another very sparsely populated area Indeed within the village itself, the group of cottages provided for railway staff almost outnumbered the remaining houses! Intended as a staging post for visitors to Selborne - the home of the naturalist Gilbert White, the location never received its share of visitors, not helped by the fact that Selborne village was a good two miles from the railhead and it is doubtful if any public transport was ever provided. Only one coal merchant is known to been based at the station, 'Ralph Trimmer', and this may only have been for a brief period between 1907 and 1911. Aside from this the majority of traffic handled would have been agricultural, with little or no specific industry near the station may well have been generated from the nearby country seat of Rotherfield Park. (Author's collection)

Looking from the south end of the up platform we see the station was built on a curve. The over bridge spanning the platforms is unusual for this line as it a steel structure rather than brick. The bridge carried the public road but was later downgraded to a footpath after the closure of the line and an extension to the former goods yard access was turned into a new public thoroughfare. (S.L.S.)

The signal box at Tisted, being sited on the outside of the curve has a good view of its area of control from those big windows. (N Simmons / H. Davis)

A down goods train passes through Tisted. (South Western Circle)

M7 No 30055 coasts into the station with a down train on the last day. (South Western Circle)

Looking back from track level. The original goods shed from here was resited to Fawley. (N Simmons / H. Davis)

Turning round we see the line curving away towards Farringdon. (N Simmons / H. Davis)

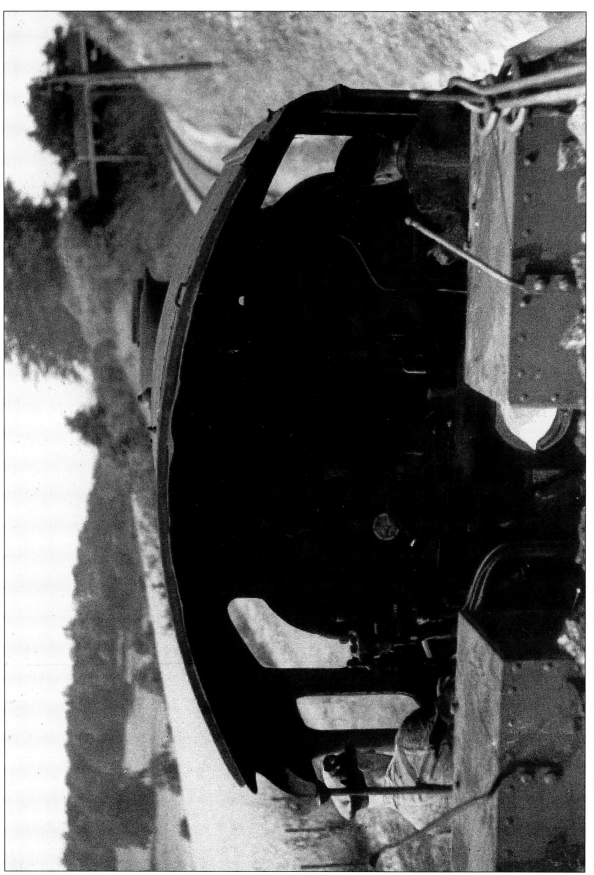

On our way to Farringdon on board Q Class No 545 we pass under a little footbridge. (South Western Circle)

FARRINGDON

Approaching Farringdon we pass the ground frame which gave access to the two sidings. (Lens)

A little further round the curve we find the short wooden platform which was provided following public demand in May 1931. (Denis Callender)

Once the train has gone we can see yet another of the sheds to house the platelayers trolley.
(N Simmons / H. Davis)

Looking back from the north end of the station shows that only one end of the platform was provided with a ramp.
(South Western Circle)

A Railway Enthusiast Club special has arrived at Farringdon, but where has the platform gone? Rumour has it that a special was sent, from Alton, down the Meon Valley line instead of over the Alps to Alresford. Is this it?
(South Western Circle)

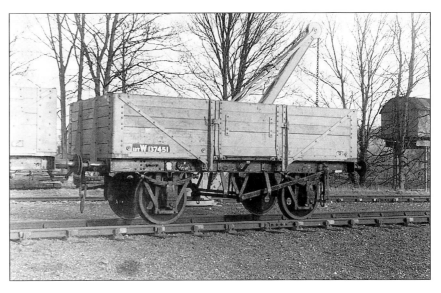

Before we leave Farringdon lets take a look in the goods yard where we find an ex GWR 13 ton open wagon No W137451. Behind the wagon can be seen the goods yard crane which were to a standard design and in the background the water tank.
(N Simmons / H. Davis)

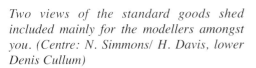

Two views of the standard goods shed included mainly for the modellers amongst you. (Centre: N. Simmons/ H. Davis, lower Denis Cullum)

Just south of Butts Junction we find a wide cab Class T9 No 30337 heading south. The embankment of the Alton to Alresford line can be seen in the background. (E C Griffiths, South Western Circle)

BUTTS JUNCTION

An early view of Butts Junction showing an Adams Class T1 in Drummond livery pulling at least a four-coach train (possibly a 4½ set which were common on this line in its early years) off the Meon Valley line to join the then double track section to Alton. In 1935 the junction was removed and the double track between here and Alton became two independent single lines. In the background can be seen the embankment carrying the Basingstoke and Alton Light Railway opened in 1901. (South Western Circle)

Another view at Butts junction, although no longer technically a junction since the tracks are now two single tracks to Alton, shows Class 700 No 30326 heading south with the 10.20am Alton to Fareham goods on 3rd February 1955. The original signal box has had its frame removed and its upper structure demolished, but a new roof has been built on the brick base to provide accommodation for the permanent way staff. (Denis Cullum)

Taken from the leading coach of a Push-Pull set heading west between Butts junction and Alton showing the widened track bed and one of the three bridges over this section. (Denis Callender)

We arrive at Alton where we find the 1865 façade little changed in the 1930's except for the addition of SOUTHERN style signage. In fact it is still much the same to this day. (S E Bolan, K Robertson)

ALTON

Looking west from the end of Alton station showing the signalling for the two parallel single lines heading towards Butts Junction and beyond.
(Denis Callender)

We end our journey, as we began, on the last day of scheduled passenger trains, with Class M7 No 30055 waiting at platform 3 to head the last down train to Fareham. The locomotive has been turned, it usually worked bunker first towards Fareham. This would also be the last journey for the locomotive on this line as, being a Fratton engine, it would be relieved by Class 700 No 30326 of Guildford shed, for the return working of the final up train, which had worked a down goods over the Meon Valley line earlier in the day. (Denis Callender)

GRADIENT PROFILE & TRACK PLANS

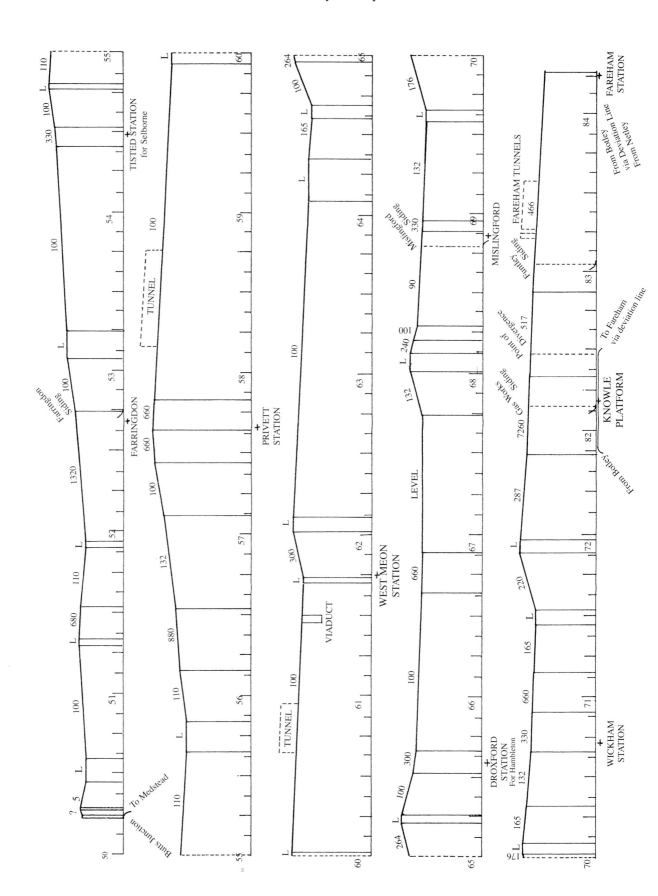

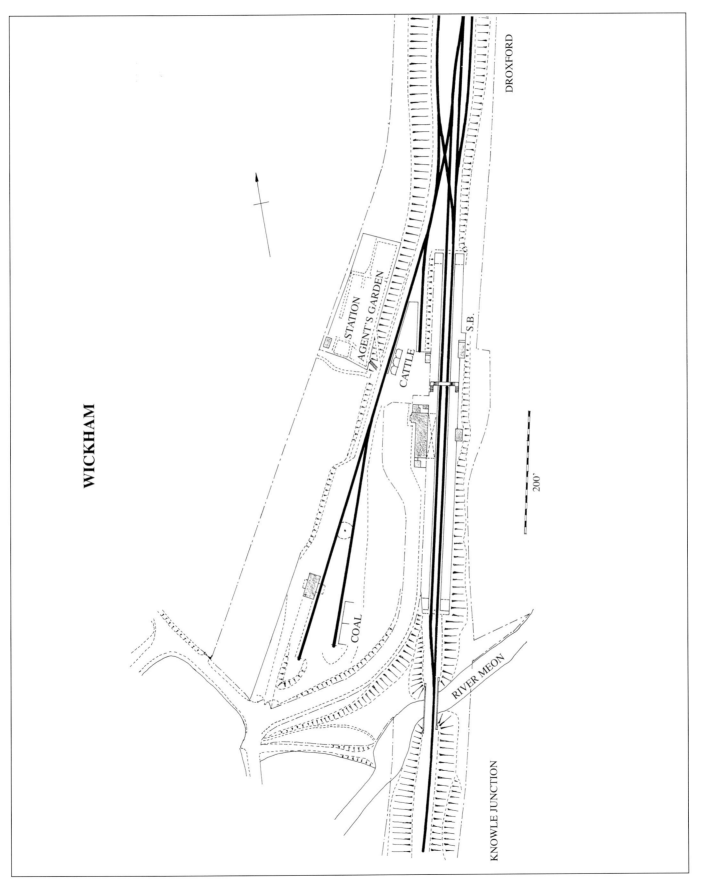

WICKHAM

STATION

AGENT'S GARDEN

CATTLE

COAL

S.B.

DROXFORD

RIVER MEON

KNOWLE JUNCTION

200'

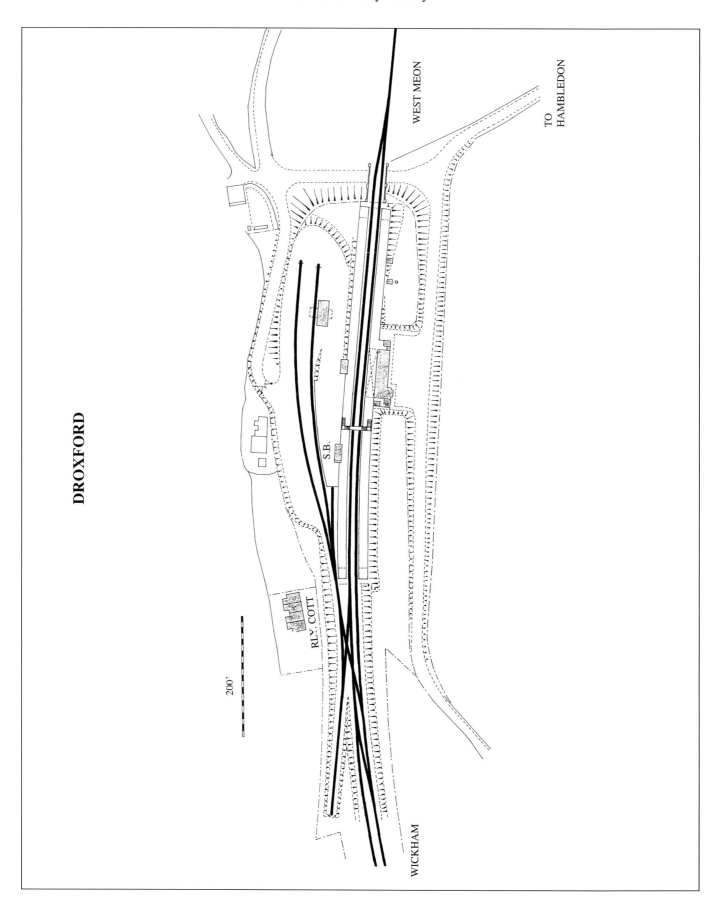

DROXFORD

WEST MEON

TO HAMBLEDON

WICKHAM

S.B.

RLY. COTT.

200'

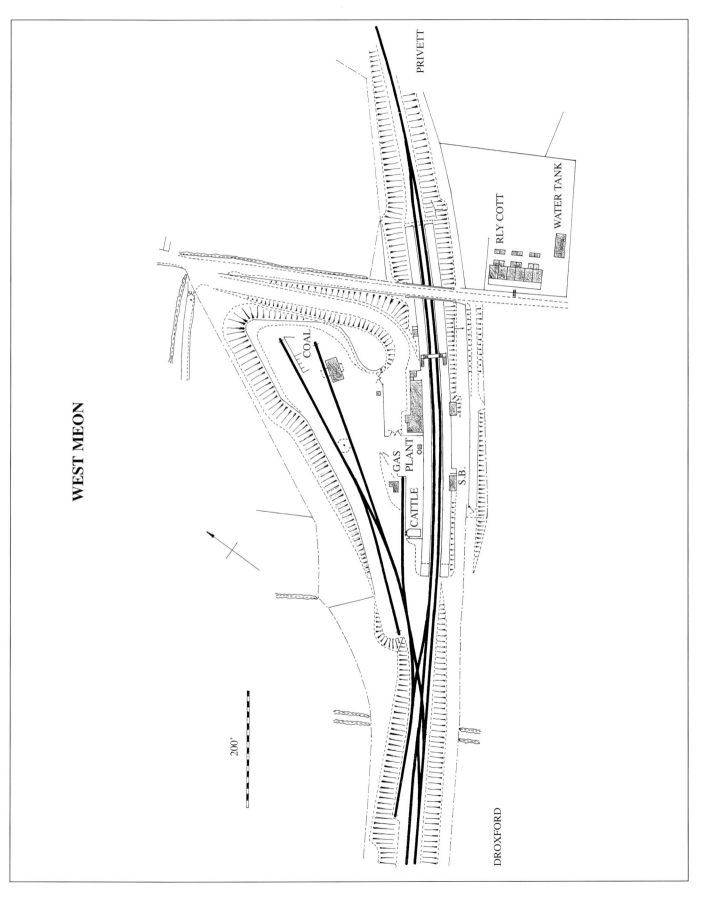

WEST MEON

PRIVETT

RLY COTT

WATER TANK

COAL

GAS PLANT

CATTLE

S.B.

DROXFORD

200'

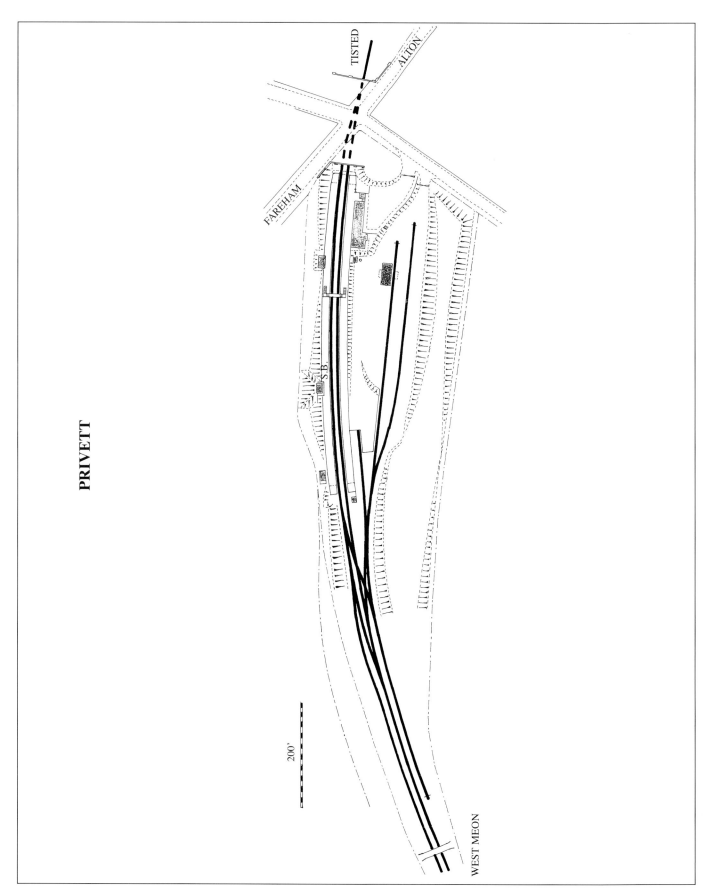

PRIVETT

TISTED

ALTON

FAREHAM

S.B.

WEST MEON

200'

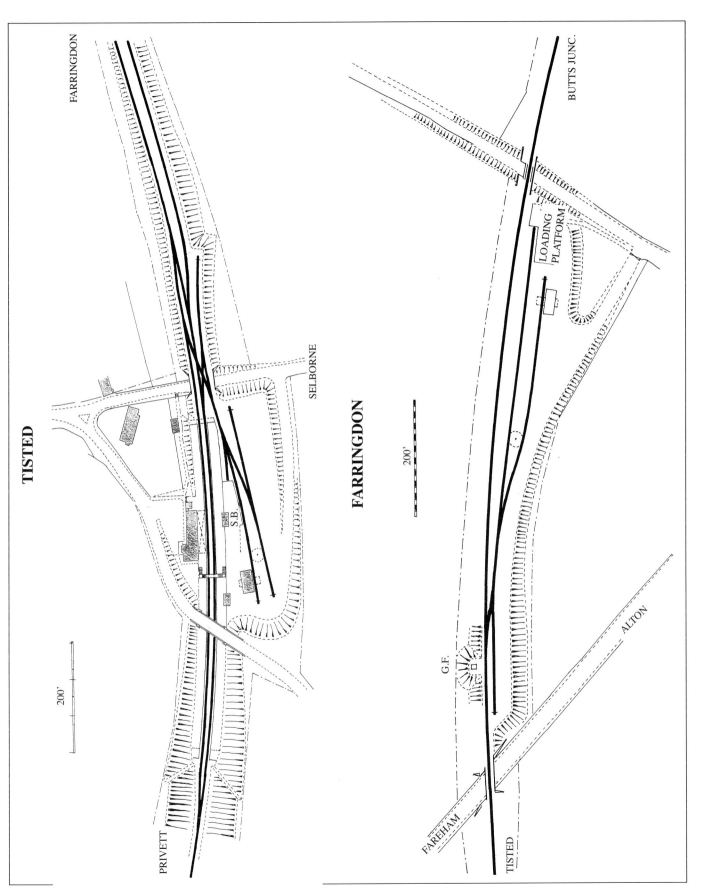

TISTED

FARRINGDON

PRIVETT

SELBORNE

S.B.

200'

FARRINGDON

BUTTS JUNC.

LOADING PLATFORM

G.F.

FAREHAM

TISTED

ALTON

200'

SOUTH WESTERN CIRCLE

The Historical Society for the London & South Western Railway

The South Western Circle, formed in 1962, is a society for railway historians and enthusiasts interested in the London and South Western Railway (LSWR).

The Society has a membership of over 500, and aims to assist and encourage members to enhance their knowledge of the LSWR and its successors with research and quarterly publication of the Circle's magazine 'The South Western Circular'.

Modelling activities have a high profile amongst the membership, which is able to draw upon the Circle's sales service of kits and components, comprehensive drawing service and limited photographic collections.

Membership Secretary:-

Colin Hooper
43, Raymond Road,
Portsmouth
PO6 4RB
or log onto www.lswr.org.uk

Back Cover:-   As the last passenger working on the line, 'The Solent Limited', heads south, hauled by Class 02 No 30200 and Class E1 No. 32694, from Mislingford on 30th April 1961, exactly a year to the day before the final closure of the Knowle Junction to Droxford section, we say good bye to the Meon Valley Railway.
(R French)